RUNNING THE
ROMAN
HOME

RUNNING THE
ROMAN
HOME

ALEXANDRA CROOM

First published 2011

The History Press
The Mill, Brimscombe Port
Stroud, Gloucestershire, GL5 2QG
www.thehistorypress.co.uk

British Library Cataloguing in Publication Data.
A catalogue record for this book is available from the British Library.

ISBN 978 0 7524 6517 3

Typesetting and origination by The History Press
Printed in Great Britain

CONTENTS

ACKNOWLEDGEMENTS

Thanks must go to all those people who have made this book possible. In particular I have to thank Paul Bidwell for his informative comments and suggestions, and Jane Croom and Katherine Croom for their work on the manuscript and index. Thanks also to the members of the re-enactment group *Cohors V Gallorum* who helped with the experiments, and various other re-enactors of all periods who have helped with discussions on their practical experience of everyday life when reconstructing the past.

1

INTRODUCTION

Books on the everyday life of the Romans usually describe getting dressed, going to the baths or to the amphitheatre, and attending evening dinner parties (often called 'banquets'), but rarely seem to discuss the more typical activities that make up most people's experience of daily life, such as doing the washing up and taking out the rubbish. Many of the activities, including making the bed or doing the dusting, are also typical of modern housework (although not necessarily the methods used to carry them out), while others, such as having to collect water from outside the house, are alien to modern western life.

Roman housework can be broken down into three elements: supply, maintenance and disposal. Supply involved bringing water into the house for drinking, cooking, washing and cleaning; bringing in fuel in the shape of firewood or charcoal for heating and cooking; grinding wheat grain to make flour for bread and spinning wool to make thread. Maintenance involved keeping the house clean from dust and dirt; emptying chamber pots and removing rubbish; washing up the dishes after meals; and washing clothes and household linens. Disposal was concerned with removing sewage, food waste, ash from the fire, and unwanted and broken items from the house.

The topic of Roman housework as a whole has not been studied in detail before. It has been discussed briefly in relation to women in Britain, and has been touched on in relation to slaves (Allason-Jones 2005, 78–81; Bradley 1994, 57–63). There have been individual studies of different aspects relating to the topic, such as supplying the army with water and firewood (Roth 1999), the work of professional fulleries and fulling methods (Bradley 2002), and rubbish disposal in relation to pottery (Peña 2007). This study attempts to look at the range of activities involved and the amount of time that had to be dedicated to them on a daily or weekly basis.

WHO DID THE WORK?

Women

For the last 200 years or so, housework has usually been considered to be women's work. This is partially due to the increasing division between workplace and home after the Industrial Revolution, with the family no longer working together in the same place as they lived. Instead, as it became more usual for the husband to go elsewhere to work, usually for an employer, the work outside the home that brought in money was seen as more important than the unpaid work of looking after the house. In Britain it was also partially due to the fact that in 1777 a tax was levied on male servants and large numbers of them lost their employment in favour of cheaper women, and as the work became more commonly identified as being women's work, it increasingly lost its status. The remaining male house servants were seen as a status symbol and were employed in more visible roles such as butler and footman.

The home was seen as a woman's domain in the Roman period, but this did not mean that women's lives revolved round housework. Columella explained the historical division of labour between the sexes by observing that as men were physically strong and naturally brave, they traditionally worked outside the home to provide food for the family. Women's timidity and natural caution made them better at looking after the food stored in the house and at rationing the food to make sure it lasted the full year (*On Farming*, 12, preface).

Columella devotes much of one volume of his treatise on the duties of the bailiff's wife, who was carrying out the traditional role of the farmer's wife (as the farmers' wives, according to him, had become too involved in pleasure seeking to bother doing the work themselves any more). Although the bailiff's wife worked in the house, her role was not primarily to carry out the housework, but to supervise those that did, who were both male and female. She had to store all the food and drink produced by the farm, inspect it regularly, and then ration and dole it out when needed. She had to store goods such as tools, weapons, clothes and valuables correctly, and be able to retrieve them instantly. She also had to supervise the preparation of the implements and wine cellar needed for the wine harvest and clean the implements used in the olive harvest.

She had to make sure that the slaves who had finished their indoor work had gone to work outside, and had to look after the sick. She supervised and checked the slaves who cleaned the bronze vessels and aired the furniture, those who worked at the loom, those who worked in the kitchen and those who were preserving food. Her work also took her outside of the house, making sure the cowsheds and managers were cleaned, checking up on the shepherds milking the sheep and counting the fleeces during shearing. The only housework mentioned in relation to her was doing wool-working with the other women on wet or rainy days when they could not work out in the fields (12.1–3; 12.8.6; 12.18.1–4; 12.52.14).

Men

It is very clear from what literary and artistic evidence survives from the Roman world that men were just as often engaged in housework as women. They are noted sweeping floors, grinding wheat, doing the washing up, cleaning clothes, fetching water and cooking. At no time is it suggested that carrying out any of these activities was unusual for them. The only common household task that they do not seem to have engaged in was spinning thread, which seems to have been almost exclusively a female occupation (although Pliny does say that spinning flax was a respectable occupation 'even for men': *Natural Histories*, 19.2.18). The heavy work involved in preparing raw wool and the skill required in weaving meant that both these tasks were considered suitable for men. In the late fourth century Claudian sarcastically describes an enemy general as someone who had 'once been a skilled wool-worker and a cunning carder, none other could so well cleanse the dirt from the fleece and fill the baskets, none other pull the thick wool over the iron teeth of the comb as he could'. It is clear this was not seen as a noble occupation as the man is described as a coward 'who sat lazily among old dames and distaffs' and who died dishonourably (*Against Eutropius II*, 383–5).

Slaves

In the Roman world generally, the division of work between who did housework and who did not was not so much between male and female, as between slave and free. It was slaves who carried out the minutiae of looking after the house, such as sweeping the floor or throwing out the slops. Even the poorest household would aspire to the ownership of a slave, although it might still mean working alongside them on household tasks. In the poem *Moretum*, a poor farmer is the first one to wake in the morning and immediately sets to work grinding some wheat; he only then wakes up his female slave and sets her to lighting the fire and heating water. The possession of only a single slave could be a cause for shame and was used as an indicator of very lowly social status, while the possession of large retinues of household slaves was seen as a status symbol by the rich, despite the drawbacks of slave ownership (Wiedermann 1981, 91–2, 94). However, a study of slave ownership amongst members of a religious association at Minturnae in about 100 BC showed that there were very few households with large numbers of slaves, with 125 out of the 127 households having no more than three slaves (*ibid.*, 100).

While a Jewish wife was responsible for domestic tasks – she had to grind flour, bake bread, wash clothes, cook food, breastfeed her child, make the bed and work wool –

she could escape doing the actual work if she brought bondswomen with her. If she brought one she did not need to do the grinding, baking or washing; if she brought two bondswomen she did not have to cook or breastfeed her child; if three she did not need to make the bed or do wool work; if four she could sit in a chair all day at leisure (*Mishnah*, Nashim, Ketuboth 5.5).

In families with such small numbers of slaves, the slaves would be expected to carry out a number of different tasks. In the comedy *The Merchant* by Plautus, the master of the household declares: 'We have no need of a female-slave except one who weaves, grinds flour, chops wood, spins thread, sweeps the house, stands a beating and has all the household meals ready every-day' (act 2, sc. 3). Whilst the list is meant for comic effect, for many slaves it must have been close to reality. On the other hand, in very rich households the tasks could be divided between a number of different people, their job titles suggesting that they only had one task to carry out; finding jobs to occupy the 400 household slaves known to have been owned by the Urban Prefect Pedanius Secundus must certainly have been made easier by sub-dividing every possible task. Roman law indicates that staff at a rural villa could include a water carrier, kitchen maid, fuller, miller, sweeper and furniture supervisor, as well as 'women who bake bread and look after the house', while tombstones belonging to members of the household of the Empress Livia record jobs such as water carrier, clothes folder, clothes mender, furniture polisher and furniture supervisor amongst the 50 surviving job titles (Bradley 1994, tables 1, 3).

The status of those engaged in housework would have been as low in the Roman period as in more modern times, although for a different reason. In the Roman world it was because it was carried out by slaves rather than because it was unpaid work performed by women. Slaves engaged purely with housework would also have been low in the servile hierarchy, as those who had been trained in specific trades or jobs, such as scribe, weaver, cobbler or musician, would have been worth more to their masters as a commodity. However, slaves engaged in domestic work must have been much more numerous than skilled slaves, as while every household would have wanted someone to fetch the water and get rid of the rubbish, they did not necessarily need a slave with a trade.

LOCATION

The nature of housework, especially that of supply, differed according to the location of the house, depending on whether it was in a small community in the country, a medium-sized town or military fortress, or one of the major cities of the empire.

Individual Rural House

Whether a massive, multi-roomed villa or small farmstead, many rural habitations were isolated and therefore self-sufficient as far as was possible. They had free and unlimited access to a source of water, not used by many, if any, other people in the immediate area. The occupants either owned land or had easy access to common land for collecting firewood and had plenty of available space for disposing of rubbish.

Small Settlements

This category includes villages, small towns and forts, where a sizeable number of people lived in close proximity. Some may have had access to their own water supply, such as a well, but most would have had to share a water source. The countryside was close enough for people to gather firewood, if they wished, but they would be competing against a large number of other people wanting to utilise the same resource. The outskirts of the settlement were close enough for the disposal of rubbish without too much inconvenience, whether it was taken there by the house owners or collected on their behalf. The disposal of sewage was more problematic than in the country and would have had an impact on the state of the settlement.

Large Cities

The problems of huge numbers of people living together in one place were enough for the authorities to take it upon themselves to deal with some of the problems of supply and disposal, such as piping water into the city to numerous public fountains and building sewers to deal with waste water and sewage. The city folk were unlikely to be able to supply themselves with fuel and would have had to buy it. Rubbish disposal was into public areas such as the streets, and again its removal had to be dealt with at a city level to some extent.

THE USE OF TECHNOLOGY

In the late first century BC or the early first century AD Antipater of Thessalonica wrote:

> rest your quern-turning hands, maidens who grind! Sleep on even when the cock's crow announces dawn, for Demeter has reassigned to the water nymphs the chores your hands performed. They leap against the very edge of the wheel,

making the axle spin, which, with its revolving cogs turns the heavy pair of porous millstones from Nisyros. (*Greek Anthology*, 9.418; trans. Oleson 1986, 151)

Despite Antipater's optimism, the number of querns found in the archaeological records show that grinding by hand remained commonplace for most households in the Roman world.

The need for investment of capital meant that many advanced technologies were initially invented under state stimulus, and only later taken up by private businesses (Wilson 2002, 32). The technologies were restricted to those businesses that could make enough money to cover the capital costs, such as using complex water-raising wheels in mines and animal-powered mills in bakeries, and therefore tended to benefit only those living in large cities, as it was only the authorities of such places that could afford the costs involved. Some of the largest watermill complexes may have been set up as part of the system for providing municipal bread doles, while the later private ventures were always set up near urban centres as only they had suitably extensive markets to make it worthwhile (*ibid.*, 14–5, 31).

Large public engineering projects also built aqueducts to provide water for bathhouses and networks of public fountains for household water requirements. In London, for example, a series of large wells used sophisticated systems of bucket chains to raise huge quantities of water (Blair *et al.* 2006). It is estimated that just one of them could provide enough water for a third of the estimated population of the city at the time, although their principal purpose may have been to provide water for the nearby bathhouse, as at the baths at Barzan, France, where a similar bucket chain was used (*ibid.*, 24, 48).

The military also took advantage of some advanced technologies, such as bringing water supplies close to or into forts and using watermills to grind wheat in large quantities (Bidwell 2007, 83, 93; Spain 2002, 55), and may well have been responsible for the spread of water-powered technology throughout the provinces (Wilson 2002, 11). The rationale is straightforward: if soldiers did not have to spend several hours every day collecting water and grinding their wheat rations, then they would have time for more military activities.

Other aspects of housework did not benefit from technological improvements. One example is spinning. Although it took five spinners to supply one weaver, and part of the huge cost of clothing came from the time involved in its production, spinning by hand continued throughout the Roman period. Why no technological advance was made in this area is unclear. In the fourth century official state weavers' workshops (*gynaecea*) were set up to provide clothing for soldiers, probably because the earlier system, by which each province had to supply a set quota of clothing, was not meeting the army's requirements (Wild 19687, 650–5). The *gynaecea* seem to have been staffed both by people working in their own homes producing a set annual output and slaves under supervision in the workshops, many of whom were probably convicts (*ibid.*, 654, 657). Even though the workshops were run by the state, and despite the constant need for large quantities of clothing, there is no evidence that the formation of these manufactories led to any technological advances, and it was to be another 1000 years before the widespread use of spinning wheels increased the rate of yarn production.

SOURCES OF EVIDENCE

Literary

Most of the texts were written by men (often, of course, of the upper classes) from the Mediterranean region, and are therefore biased towards the materials and methods used in that area. However, they can provide unrivalled information about the physical activities themselves, such as how tables were wiped down, as well as the materials or ingredients that were used in, for example, cleaning metalwork or washing clothes. However, the authors usually had little interest in housework as such, so when Pliny mentions that tamarisk trees are used to make brooms it was because he was interested in the plant and its uses, not because he was writing about housework.

Details of some of the more important sources are listed in the appendix.

Archaeological

The archaeological evidence provides information regarding the disposal of rubbish, from the huge dumps of urban settlements to the scatter of broken pottery and animal bones found on all sites. Where the environmental conditions are right, excavation can even produce some of the tools used in housework, from scraps of cloth to scrubbing brushes to wooden buckets found at the bottom of wells, items which are so rarely shown in art. Archaeology also reveals the scale and sophistication of the large engineering projects used to bring water, in particular, to large urban centres.

Artistic

As most housework was carried out by slaves, it did not have much appeal for those commissioning art and so is very rarely depicted. Clothes washing is shown because a professional fuller wanted his business activities recorded, and collecting water is only shown as part of the New Testament incident of Jesus and the Samaritan woman. The traditional role of women as woolworkers meant that the equipment needed for spinning is often shown on tombstones, or else the deceased is shown holding it, but images of women actually spinning are uncommon. When they are shown, it is often in mythological scenes such as the Fates, or Hercules when he was disguised as a woman. A rare and intriguing exception to the lack of artistic depictions of housework is a scene showing slaves at work in the kitchen on the massive funerary monument at Igel in Germany.

COMPARISONS

Many of the activities that made up housework in the Roman world are very foreign to a modern western way of life, but are remarkably similar to household tasks carried out routinely until the start of the twentieth century, and which are still performed today in many developing countries. Later parallels have been cited to show non-western, pre-twenty-first-century approaches to the tasks. For example, it is difficult to imagine doing the washing up without using hot water and washing-up liquid, but since the liquid was only invented in the 1950s comparatively few people have ever actually used this method, while using sand has an extremely long and widespread history.

2

SUPPLY: COLLECTING WATER

A nyone building or buying a house in the Roman period had to consider the problems of organising their own supply of water. Some people might rely on public resources, such as a nearby river or spring in the countryside or street fountains within a town or city. Others might prefer to have greater control by having their own source of water, such as a well or cistern, or, if they lived in a city or large town, paying for the luxury of water piped into their house.

For the majority of people, collecting water involved having to leave their house several times a day, either simply walking outside to a well close by or having to make a much longer trek to a public fountain or to a local spring or river. Although this might be inconvenient (no doubt especially in winter), later parallels suggest that sometimes it was seen as an advantage, with women in particular finding it an excuse to leave the house and have the opportunity to talk to others. Fetching water from outside the house has been a daily occupation in Britain until comparatively recently: piped water inside houses was not common until the late nineteenth or early twentieth century, and even as late as 1934 a study of working-class areas in London revealed that in half of the houses under consideration water still had to be collected from outside the home, either from a tap on a landing, across a yard or down and up three flights of stairs (Davidson 1986, 7, 31).

Water could be collected from a number of different locations; from natural sources such as rivers, ponds and springs; from man-made underground structures such as wells and cisterns, and from built features that required water to be directed into them, such as tanks and fountains. The Romans were very much aware of the different taste and quality of water available, depending on both the local geology and how fast or sluggish the water flowed, and on occasion used different sources for different purposes (cf. Pliny, *Natural Histories*, 31.28). Their ideal was moving water with no appreciable taste or smell, and which did not produce any muddy sediment when boiled (*ibid.*, 31.22; 23).

SOURCES

Surface Water

Water could be collected from any convenient river, stream or lake, although the quality of the water could vary considerably depending on source, speed and the geography of the area it passed through (see fig. 1a). Pliny observed that 'the taste of rivers is usually variable, owing to the great difference in river beds. For waters vary with the land over which they flow, and with the juices of the plants they wash' (*Natural Histories*, 31.29.52).

The water could contain sediment, mud or organic material which had to be removed before it could be used for cooking or drinking, the simplest method being simply to let it stand for a while before use. When the water was piped into settlements via aqueducts it often passed through deep settling tanks where it had the chance to stand for a while, the sediment dropping to the bottom. The River Anio was used as the source for two aqueducts in Rome, but it was a very sandy river and a tank on the route of the Anio Novus aqueduct was found to be full of pea-sized pebbles that had settled out of it (Hodge 1992, 124). In this case the water seems to have been used for watering gardens rather than for drinking.

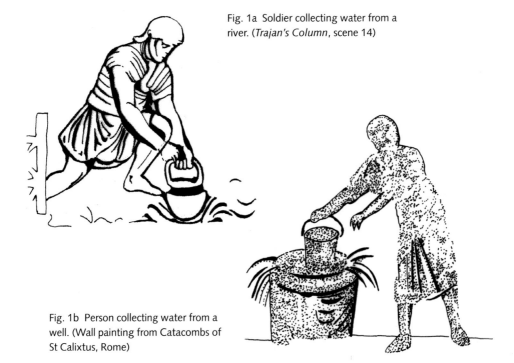

Fig. 1a Soldier collecting water from a river. (*Trajan's Column*, scene 14)

Fig. 1b Person collecting water from a well. (Wall painting from Catacombs of St Calixtus, Rome)

Springs

Springs form when a water-bearing stratum comes to the ground surface, such as on a hillside, and the water bubbles out naturally. They were popular sources of water (see plate 1). Spring water is often flavoured by the chemicals in the stone through which it has percolated and had a taste that could not be removed, but it was often preferred to surface-water sources as it at least looked clean and fresh, and in an age before the microscope, appearance was an important indicator of health. When Pliny described the glories of his Laurentine villa, one of the advantages he noted was that: 'wherever you dig you come upon water at once which is pure and not in the least brackish' (Pliny, *Letters*, 2.17.25).

Wells

One of the most common sources of water was the well, where a shaft was dug down to reach the water table below ground. Pliny was of the opinion that the most commendable water came 'from wells, as I see they are generally used in towns, but they should be those the water of which is kept in constant motion by frequent withdrawals' (*Natural Histories*, 31.23.38). Wells had to be dug, and therefore involved an initial cost not necessary when collecting water from rivers, ponds or springs. An *aquilex*, a person with experience of finding water, was hired to choose the best place to site the well, and then a large inverted cone was dug until they hit water (*ibid.*, 31.27–8). A shaft was built in the centre of the cone, which was then back-filled with soil. The well shaft could be made of timber, stone or both. Masonry wells were usually circular in shape, as were some timber-lined wells when old barrels were used to form the lining, stacked up on each other with the tops and bottoms knocked out. Wells lined with wooden planks were more usually square or rectangular, for ease of construction (Adam 2005, fig. 547).

There was not one typical size of well, as each one depended on local conditions and the depth of the water table. The usual range was between 0.5m to 2m in diameter and anything from 3m to 25m in depth (Hodge 1992, 53). In England, wells over 15m are not uncommon; a well in the Forum at Lincoln was 3m wide and 15m deep; one of the wells of the villa at Dalton Parlours was 16m deep; and the well at the temple at Pagans Hill, Somerset, was 17m deep (Jones 2003, 115, fig. 12.2; Wrathmell and Nicholson 1990, 195; Rahtz *et al.* 1958, fig. 20). If necessary, wells could be much deeper, such as an 80m well at Poitiers in France, but apart from the difficulties of digging such a well, when completed more time and energy was required to bring the water to the top, making deep wells unpopular with users.

The top of the well usually had a low wall built round it to stop people and animals falling in, and sometimes also had a removable lid. The most common method of collecting the water was by using a bucket or pottery vessel attached to the end of a rope. At its most basic, the container was raised by pulling the rope over the edge of the wellhead. However, collecting water from a well of any depth was not particularly easy, requiring the repeated lifting of not just the weight of the water, but also the weight of the bucket and of the rope up the full height of the well. Therefore, simple machinery was commonly used to reduce the effort involved. The rope could be wrapped several times round a windlass on a horizontal bar built across the top of the well or could be passed through a pulley. The advantage of this system was that the container was kept away from the walls of the well, avoiding any snagging against rough projections on the inner wall and reducing damage to the rope or container. The rope was also being pulled down rather than up, a noticeably easier action (Hodge 1992, 55).

At public wells the container for drawing the water and for carrying it away were usually one and the same, with no vessel left permanently attached to the rope. In the New Testament incident of the woman of Samaria, a woman comes to a well with a jar to collect some water. Jesus has to ask her for a drink of water since the well, as the woman observes, was deep, and he had no means of drawing any himself. To her confusion, Jesus then talks metaphorically of a 'living water' and says that anyone who drinks it will never be thirsty again. The woman promptly asks for some of this water so that she would not be stuck with the chore of water-collecting ever again (John, 4:7–30).

Early Christian illustrations of this scene show a variety of well designs, including the reused top of a large pottery storage vessel (see fig. 2a; the use of the windlass shows that it cannot simply be a large *dolium*, a man-high-sized pottery vessel, sunk into the ground and used to store water temporarily). The top half of a *dolium* was used as a wellhead in a house at Pompeii, while at least six *dolia* stacked on top of each other were used as a well lining at a site at Piammiano, Italy (Peña 2007, 196, fig. 7.1). Most of the other illustrations show simple lifting mechanisms, consisting of two uprights joined by a horizontal bar that carried the windlass, although the method of turning the windlass is not always shown. An image on a decorated box from Brescia shows cross-shaped handles on either side of the frame (see fig. 2d).

A deep well without any means of reaching the water also troubled Ammianus Marcellinus and fellow soldiers when he was making his way to Antioch after escaping from the siege of Amida in 359:

> since the heat had caused us parching thirst, for a long time we went slowly about looking for water. We fortunately found a deep well, but it was neither possible to go down it because of its depth, nor had we any ropes, so, taught by extreme need, we tore up the linen clothes we wore into long rags and made them into a great rope. At the very end of this we tied the cap that one of us wore under his helmet, and when we let down the rope it sucked up the water like a sponge, it readily quenched the thirst that tormented us. (*Histories*, 19.8)

Figs 2a–d Illustrations of the Samaritan woman collecting water from the well: a. Wall painting from Catacombs under the Via Latina, Rome; b. Ivory panel, probably from Egypt, in Fitzwilliam Museum, Cambridge; c. Mosaic, Basilica of S. Apollinare Nuovo, Ravenna; d. Jacob meeting Rachel at a well: ivory casket. (The Brescia Lipsanotheca)

Wells were just as common in towns and cities as in the countryside. Frontinus pointed out that 'for 441 years from the foundation of the City [of Rome], the Romans were satisfied with the use of such waters as they drew from the River Tiber, from wells and from springs' (*On Aqueducts*, 1.4). Excavations within London have revealed over 50 so far, some of which seem to have been for public use (Williams 2003, 244, 248).

Cistern

A cistern was a large, lined tank built at or just below ground level that was fed from above (for example, by collecting rainwater) rather than below like a well. The Romans did not have guttering under the roof eaves in the modern manner, but the rainwater could be collected after it had drained from the roof, either by having a cistern immediately below it or by collecting surface run-off. In *atrium* houses, the shallow pool (*impluvium*) beneath the roof opening had two drains, one leading to a cistern and one to the street; by closing off one or the other drain the water could be kept for use or directed out on to the street (Jansen 2007, 259). The cistern mouth was by the side of the pool, usually protected by an upstanding cylinder, through which the water could be drawn (see fig. 3). A study of a sample of *atrium* houses in Pompeii has, in fact, revealed that these cistern-mouth covers (puteals) were most commonly found in the peristyle, often between the columns or in the surrounding veranda, or in secondary courtyards and their entrances, rather than in the *atrium* (Allison 2004, 86, 90, 110). Situated in these positions they would be covering cisterns which collected rainwater from open guttering round the edges of the courtyards (Jansen 2007, fig. 16.2; Adam 2005, figs 548–9).

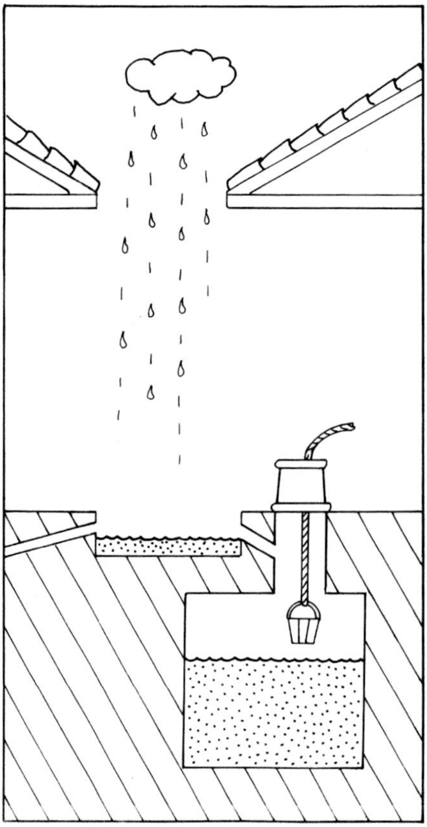

Cisterns were particularly common in hot, dry countries, where water was scarce and could not be wasted, and in arid provinces cisterns were sometimes built to serve entire cities (Hodge 1992, 60). A domestic cistern might hold 30m³ of water, while 12 public examples in Cherchel, Algeria, ranged in capacity from 30 to 130m³. Cisterns used to store water brought in by aqueducts could hold up to 25,000m³ (Hodge 1992, 62). Small cisterns had a covered wellhead for drawing up the water by means of a rope, while large cisterns usually had stairs

Fig. 3 Water cistern in an *atrium*-type house (after Jansen 2007). The *impluvium* has a drain leading to the cistern (to the right) and a second overflow drain at a higher level (to the left). The cistern entrance is protected by a puteal.

leading down to the water for collection (Adam 2005, fig. 573). As the water was static, it was not necessarily fresh when it was used, but any water was better than none. Pliny recorded that some doctors recommended cistern water, as it was particularly 'light', having risen up into the air as rainwater, but Pliny himself thought that 'no other water contains more slime or disgusting insects', and that it became putrid quickly and was 'the worse water to stand a voyage' (*Natural Histories*, 31.21.32–4).

Piped Water

Due to the heavy demand for water, some urban centres had to bring water in from sources outside the immediate area via aqueducts in order to make sure they had a constant supply. Rome had a total of 11 aqueducts to supply its needs, but most cities could make do with just one. They were useful for supplying the huge quantities of water required for baths, but as they were expensive engineering projects some cities survived without one. Pliny records that the people of the city of Nicomedia wasted 3 million *sesterces* on one attempt to build an aqueduct and a further 200,000 on a second failed attempt. As well as carrying water to baths, they were used to supply a network of public drinking fountains, where the inhabitants could collect as much water as they required.

The best example of a surviving water distribution system is at Pompeii. The water brought in by an aqueduct was fed into a large tank built into a structure called a *castellum*. Three pipes led out of this central reservoir, and they have often been interpreted, using literary evidence, as being pipes for the baths and theatres, for the public fountains and for private use. This division, however, would require an unrealistic three separate networks of pipes which for much of the time would have followed exactly the same route, with the result that one pipe would serve a private house while a separate pipe on a different system would serve the public fountain immediately outside it, and a third would lead to a theatre only a few metres away on the other side of the street. It seems more likely that the three pipes in the *castellum* simply served different parts of the town (Hodge 1992, 322).

The main pipes lead to secondary *castella* and then, through a network of smaller pipes, to individual customers. In Pompeii 12 or 14 such *castella* have been identified, consisting of lead tanks set on piers *c*.6m tall in order to help control the water pressure (*ibid.*, 300, 304). Lead pipes ran down the side of the piers and into a distribution network under the street or pavement.

At Colchester the water system was distributed through wooden pipes held together by iron collars (Crummy 1984, 26–8, figs 107–9). Here the fortress and much of the subsequent town were about 15m above the water table so wells were only dug in low-lying areas and most of the settlement's water requirements had to be supplied by water either pumped up from nearby springs or brought in from some distance by aqueduct.

Excavations at Balkerne Lane revealed the remains of four wooden pipes laid side by side in a single trench; the water pipes must have been part of a pressurised system which would have required a *castellum*, possibly positioned to the east of the town wall, close to where later reservoirs and water towers were built (*ibid.*, 26–8; fig. 108).

Public Fountains

At Pompeii the pipes fed into the stone tanks of the public fountains, one of which was often set at the base of the pier of the secondary *castellum*. The stone tanks were rectangular, approximately 1.8m by 1.5m by 0.8m deep (see plate 2). The pipe was fed through a hole in a slightly taller stone set at the head of the tank, which was often decorated with a carving. Examples include the heads of deities, lions or bulls, theatrical masks, flowers and a cornucopia. The system was designed for a constant flow of water, so a notch was cut in one wall to channel the overflow away when the tank filled completely, such as overnight when no one was collecting water (Adam 2005, figs 595–9). A completely full tank held in the region of 886 litres of water, although the worn stones near the fountains show that people preferred to collect the water from under the outflow in order to have the freshest water possible (*ibid.*, 259). Forty-three public water fountains have been uncovered so far at Pompeii, placed approximately 100m apart. It has been calculated that the majority of the town's inhabitants would have had to walk no more than 50m to fetch their water, only a couple of minutes' walk (see fig. 4).

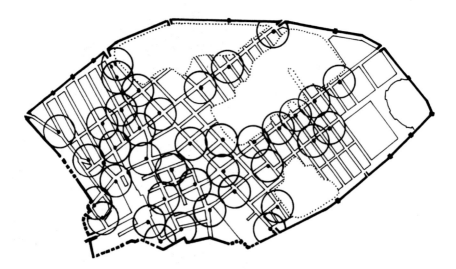

Fig. 4 Location of public fountains in Pompeii. The circles represent a 50m radius from each fountain. (After Hodge 1992)

Piped Water Inside Houses

Those who wanted water brought into their houses had to pay for the privilege, so only a very small section of society made use of it. At Pompeii only 124 out of 1000 excavated properties had piped water (Jones and Robinson 2005, 699), and there is at least one example of a pipe leading to a water tank on an upper storey of a private house where it was then distributed to a number of local properties, probably as an example of neighbours grouping together to pay a single fee (Hodge 1992, 326). As piped water was a status symbol, having it in the house was not intended to make life easier for the slaves in the kitchen; the water was used instead for bath suites and features such as fountains that could be seen by visitors (Jones and Robinson 2005, 702).

In Rome itself, individual pipes were connected to the tank in a secondary *castellum* by a bronze fitting (one which could not be distorted as lead could be) so that customers could not get more water than they were entitled to. The size of the fitting was all that controlled the amount of water, which could easily fluctuate according to the level of water in the tank, the rate of flow, the state of the aqueduct and so on (Hodge 1992, 295).

After reaching the house, the water was fed into smaller gauge pipes which took it to wherever it was required. The pipes were not always hidden away as in a modern house, since they were part of the status symbol of piped water. If the house had a bath suite, this would have been the most important destination, followed by gardens or courtyards, where the water was used in decorative channels, pools and fountains. The kitchen was not a common destination. Sinks, although sometimes found in the counters of inns, were not usual in private kitchens, although there were sometimes larger storage tanks. Water was rarely piped to upper floors, so those living in apartments above ground level could not benefit from private sources.

A study of the House of the Vestals in Pompeii (Jones and Robinson 2005) has shown that before it acquired piped water, it was supplied from five underground cisterns filled with rainwater, and did not have any water displays in its gardens. When piped water was introduced, it was used only for decorative purposes and to supply the bath suite. The cisterns remained in use, presumably for domestic purposes, but the overflow from the pipes was not collected in them and simply flowed out into the street drains (although slaves may have collected water for domestic use from the water features). When the supply of piped water ended after the earthquake in AD 62, the water features in the house were removed.

In some houses the water pipe outflow was found in a central position in the house, such as the peristyle, perhaps located over a drain. Water could be collected from this one point and taken to wherever in the house it was required. As the water flowed constantly, there was less need for taps, but examples of taps of both the 'discharge' and 'stop-cock' type have been found. A discharge tap is one situated at the end of a pipe and usually kept closed until water is required (as in a modern kitchen tap), while a stop-cock tap is found in the middle of a length of pipe, used to stop the water flowing.

Unlike modern taps, the design of Roman taps meant that they tended to be either fully open or fully closed. Due to their form, larger ones had to have a rectangular loop instead of a handle, to be used with a removable key or wrench, although smaller ones used on narrow-gauge pipes were probably turned by hand (Hodge 1992, 323–4). It is not known where discharge taps were used in a domestic system, but as constant flow was typical (and required for waste disposal) they were unlikely to have been common. About 40 examples, of all types, are known from Pompeii.

COLLECTING THE WATER

Collecting water would have been the responsibility of a slave in all but the very poorest households which either had no slaves or whose slaves were employed in more skilled labour, leaving members of the family to carry out the task. The evidence suggests both men and women collected water, although where it was their sole job men were preferred for their ability to carry more (the figure of the water carrier – *Aquarius* – is found in both Roman and modern zodiacs). Collecting water was seen as a fundamental chore, so when urban properties were left as legacies the law decreed that 'doorkeepers … or gardeners, or valets and water-carriers who worked only in the house will be included' as part of the general fittings of the house necessary for its continued upkeep, rather than as part of the slave household that could be moved to other properties (*Digest*, 33.7.12.42).

Others in cities found it more convenient to pay people to bring them water. Diocletian's *Edict of Maximum Prices* of c.AD 300 sets the wages of a water carrier, including maintenance, at 25 *denarii* for a full day's work, which was the same price as a farm worker and more expensive than a shepherd, but half the cost of a skilled workman such as a blacksmith or baker. Water could also be sold, although this was perhaps only when the water was considered special, such as having medicinal properties. A relief from a tomb in Ostia shows the shop of the water seller Lucifer, complete with a large water container and shelves hung with water jugs and a customer at the counter (see fig. 5).

Water was collected in buckets or pottery jars. The buckets could usually hold more, but the narrow mouths of the jars often meant less water was lost through slopping. The chore could easily be wet and unpleasant, with the well rope (if used) dripping with water and the vessels wet on the outside from being dipped in the water. The area round the well or water tank was likely to be continually damp from spilt water or

Fig. 5 Tombstone of Lucifer the water seller, from Ostia, tomb 30.

overflow, and churned up from the number of people using it. Images of water being collected from wells sometimes show water dripping down the side of the bucket or splashing over the top (see figs 1b, 2c). Having filled the vessel, it was then necessary to carry it back home, which might have to be repeated several times a day. It was a monotonous task that had to be carried out every single day.

In the play *The Rope* by Plautus, a rural householder who had dug a well 'at our own cost with our own tools' was tired of the people visiting a nearby shrine of Venus asking for water and borrowing things: 'They're for ever coming to my house for water, or fire, or dishes, or a knife, or a spit or a pot to cook tripe in, or something. It would seem, in short, that I got my kitchenware and well for Venus, not myself.' The man, however, does not mind giving water to his next door neighbour, the priestess, and when a pretty woman from her house asks to have her water jar filled, his slave Sceparnio is only too happy to help and for once enjoys the experience: 'What fun was drawing this up! The well didn't seem anything like as deep as it used to be. Why it was no work at all drawing this up.' He is not so satisfied when he finds the woman has disappeared and he has to carry the water jar to their house: 'A nice job I've struck, if I've actually got to go ahead and lug their water for 'em' (act 1, 134; act 2, sc. 4–5).

In another play by Plautus, a slave threatens a fellow slave with the job of water carrier when they go into the country to their master's villa. While the threat is exaggerated the unpleasant nature of the job is implicit:

> You shall be provided with just one amphora, and one path, one spring, one bronze pot [for boiling the water] and eight *dolia* [the man-high-sized jars], and if they are not constantly full, I'll give you your fill of whip-marks. I'll make you carry water until you have such a beautiful crook in your back that they can use you for a horse's crupper. (*Casina*, 120)

Buckets

Buckets were made of wooden staves held together with iron bands and with an iron handle (see figs 2, 6). The handles sometimes had a distinctive small bend, sometimes forming a complete circle, in the centre to hold the well rope in position to stop the bucket tilting and spilling the water as it was raised (Hodge 1992, fig. 25).

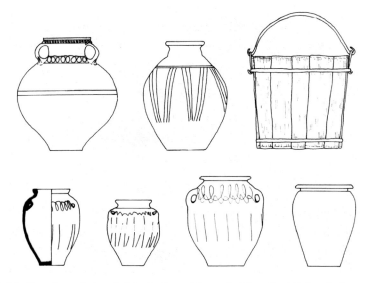

Fig. 6 Selection of vessels found at the bottom of the well of the villa at Dalton Parlours.

Water Jars

According to Varro 'water-jars (*urnae*) got their name from the fact that they dive (*urninant*) in the drawing of water', although modern scholars suggest the name was a derivative of *urina*, when this still meant 'water' rather than specifically 'urine' (*On the*

Latin Language, 5.126; Kent 1938, 120). Images in art frequently show them as large vessels with two handles (see fig. 2a; plate 1).

The best evidence for the types of containers used to collect water come from examples found within wells themselves. The excavations at Dalton Parlours, West Yorkshire, revealed a villa complex of at least 11 buildings occupied over a period of about 150 years. Amongst these there was a principal building with mosaics, an aisled building with both domestic and agricultural accommodation, and one, or possibly two, separate bathhouses, although the exact details of the other buildings are lost due to later damage. The excavations revealed two wells, although as only one was fully investigated it is not known if they were in contemporary use. Both were positioned very close to buildings which appeared to include bath suites.

Well 1 was *c*.2.2m in diameter and 16m deep, with a water level approximately 11.5m below ground level. There were four postholes round the well, either for the lifting mechanism or some form of cover; the excavators were unsure if there had been a stone building round the well that had been destroyed by ploughing (Wrathmell and Nicholson 1990, 195). The well contained five substantially complete wooden buckets and fragments of at least 11 others, plus four complete pottery vessels and 22 more that were over 70 per cent complete (see fig. 6). In total, there were 15 examples of counter-sunk, lug-handled jars and 20 jars of calcite-gritted ware.

Handled jars have been found at the bottom of a number of wells (Sumpter 1990, 244) and were clearly commonly used for drawing water. The handles are recessed into the body of the jar to make them less vulnerable to damage. One of the Dalton Parlour examples still had a bit of cord attached to it, and a number had abrasions round the girth, and chipped rims and handles suggestive of damage from the well lining or wellhead. The calcite-gritted jars had heavy sooting on the shoulders and under the rims, and calcareous deposits on the interior, and had been used for boiling water.

The lowest 1.5m fill of the well was considered to have collected during the life of the well, and contained five substantially complete vessels and a bucket. Above 1.5m the fill was considered to be a deliberate infilling, when the containers used for drawing and collecting water were thrown down the well. This consisted of four wooden buckets and the fragments of many others, two complete lug-handled jars and substantial pieces of 14 more, and four nearly complete calcite-gritted ware jars and large parts of 15 others. The large number of buckets and pottery vessels present, and the fact that most of them were available to be thrown into the deliberate infilling of the well in one operation, suggests that they were stored somewhere close to the well, and were expected to be in use at the same time, perhaps associated with the bath suite.

The villa at Rudston in East Yorkshire also had a well to supply its water. The villa had been built sometime in the third century over an Iron Age settlement whose nearest source of running water had been *c*.1000m away, so a large well 30m deep and 2.8m in diameter was dug for the villa (Stead 1980, 26). The well was close to a bath suite, but the presence of three water troughs in its filling that had presumably been set up near the wellhead suggests it was also used for watering livestock, and the distance of any other running water for domestic use means the well must have been used to supply all the settlement's water needs. Although the top part of the well was stone-lined, there was no evidence that this continued above ground, and it is possible that the wellhead was simply boarded over, with a trap door for access. At the very bottom of the well were fragments of at least two hand buckets and pieces of three or four buckets of a more robust design with pivots for attaching to an iron frame connected to a chain. One of these buckets could be reconstructed as being 30cm in diameter and 40cm high, with an approximate capacity of 19 litres. The use of a heavy iron chain in such a deep well would create problems raising the water; it has been calculated that the chain and a full bucket would weigh almost 100kg (equivalent to a 16-stone man) when it was at water level. It would require at least two people, possibly four, to wind it up, so it is possible that a two-bucket system was used, where one bucket being lowered helped to counterbalance the bucket being raised (Pacitto 1980, 114). Some time after the deposition of the buckets there was a long period of disuse, and when the well came back into use, pottery jars seem to have been preferred for collecting the water, with about 22 examples being found in the upper layers, as compared to three in the lowest ones.

CARRYING THE WATER

Whilst most artistic evidence shows only one vessel being carried (cf. plate 2), a humorous mosaic depicting a pigmy water carrier shows him with two containers hanging over either end of a rod he carries over his shoulders, which may have been a more common method for those supplying large quantities of water (Clarke 2003, fig. 123). Literary evidence refers to water jars being carried both on the shoulder and on the head (Propertius, *Elegies*, 4.11.28; Ovid, *Fasti*, 3.14).

QUANTITY OF WATER

The quantity of water that needed to be collected would have varied from household to household, according to the distance it had to be carried, who was doing the carrying, and the wealth of the people involved.

Table 1: Average Quantity of Water Used, Litres per Head per Day (after Davidson 1986)

1850	Water collected from public source (in Paisley)	6
1970	WHO minimum required to sustain life (in developing countries)	7
1850	Working classes (in Stirling)	9
1875	Rural areas	up to 18
1970	WHO water collected from public sources (developing countries)	27
1850	General Board of Health recommended consumption	27–32
1830	Average consumption in urban area (Nottingham)	32
1850	Middle class (in Stirling)	up to 55
1970	WHO average (in developing countries)	up to 55
1978	Domestic piped water in urban area (Glasgow)	227
1978	Developed country (America)	327

Table 1 shows the quantity of water used in more modern households. It is likely that many households in the Roman world used an amount towards the lower range shown in the table; clothes were probably washed in running water outside the house wherever possible, and those who had access to public or private baths probably did not need much water for daily washing.

To give an idea of what was involved some simple calculations can be made. Taking 7 litres (WHO minimum requirements), a *contubernium* of eight soldiers living and messing together would need to provide themselves with 56 litres of water every day. Using a wooden bucket like the one found in the well at Dalton Parlours (see fig. 6) that could hold approximately 11.3 litres, they would need to make five trips every day to their water source. If they used one of the pots found in the same well, the larger examples of which could only hold about 6.5 litres, the soldiers would have to make nine trips. Taking 18 litres per head (maximum use in rural areas in 1875) as the figure, the soldiers would require a daily total of 144 litres. This would require 13 trips using the bucket or 22 with the pottery vessel. The number of trips could, of course, be reduced by carrying two containers at once. However, water is not particularly lightweight, especially when carried over a distance; the full bucket would weigh over 12kg and the pot over 8.5kg. Women in the developing world carry about an average of 13.5 to 16 litres per trip, weighing up to 16kg, excluding the weight of the container (Davidson 1986, 14).

The amount of time soldiers spent collecting water would have been reduced in those forts where an aqueduct was used to bring water to the fort itself. Often they were used to bring water to the baths positioned outside the fort (Bidwell 2007, 93–4), but in some cases the water came inside the fort. At South Shields fort there is a large inscription recording bringing in a 'supply of water for the use of the soldiers of the

Fifth Cohort of Gauls' (*RIB I* 1060), with the settling tank for removing silt from the water positioned by the side of one of the roads following the line of the fort wall (Dore and Gillam 1979, 38–9; fig. 11). The time taken to collect water would have been greatly reduced if the soldiers just had to walk across the fort to get their water, rather than having to leave the fort for it.

TIME TAKEN

The time it took to bring the water home depended on how much was to be collected and the distance to the water source. In Tanzania, even urban households can spend up to two and a half hours per day collecting their water, while in Nepal 62 per cent of rural household take an average of two hours a day to collect the full amount required, or one hour if they cut their water requirements down to the minimum (Anon 1999, 166; Loughran and Pritchett 1997, table 5). The amount needed could vary from day to day, depending on what it was to be used for. In India the water requirements per person per day, excluding water for cleaning the house or watering animals, have been identified as:

Use	Litres
Drinking water	5
Daily bathing	12
Hand-washing before and after meals	4
Cleaning teeth	1
Toilet, including hand-washing	1
Washing clothes	10
Cooking	1
Washing vegetables	1
Washing utensils	5
Total	**40**

Every 7 to 10 days a further 30 litres were required for cleaning the house. When those collecting the water found the task too 'tiring and painful', they would carry only enough for drinking and cooking (7 litres) and wash themselves, their clothing and the utensils at the water source (Khanna and Khanna 2006, table 3.5; 18).

STORING WATER

After the water had been collected, it had to be stored until required. Sometimes it was poured into storage jars or water tanks close to, but outside, the house. Pottery or bronze vessels were filled at this storage point to bring the water inside the house. In other houses the water was kept inside. In the first century the author Varro describes:

> a table for vessels, rectangular ... It was called an *urnarium,* because it was the piece of furniture in the kitchen on which by preference they set and kept the water-jars (*urnae*) filled with water. From this even now the place in front of the bath where the urn-table is wont to be placed is called an *urnarium.* (*On the Latin Language,* 5.126)

In Pompeii some kitchens had small built-in masonry tanks that either had to be filled by bucket or, very occasionally, by the house's piped water supply. This meant there was a supply of water immediately to hand for use in the kitchen or to flush the nearby toilet (Jansen 1997, 130).

BOILING WATER

Even after the water had been collected and stored, it was not necessarily ready to drink, as many households then boiled the water. Pliny, for example, noted that 'it is agreed that all water is more serviceable when boiled ... It purifies bad water to boil it down to one half' (*Natural Histories,* 31.23.40). In a legal discussion about what is included in the 'fittings' of a villa left as a legacy (those items necessary to make sure the place can be run properly) it was agreed that 'the bronze vessel in which new wine is boiled, concentrated must is made, and water for the household to drink and wash in is prepared, are included' (*Digest,* 33.7.12.10). Likewise:

> we say that pots and pans are included in the 'fittings' of a farm, because without them food cannot be cooked. Nor is there much difference between pots and the bronze vessel which hangs over the fire; in the latter, water is boiled for drinking; in the former, food is cooked. But if the bronze vessel is included in the 'fittings', the water-jars, with which water is poured into the bronze vessel, are placed in the same category, and so eventually each next item is linked to the one before to infinity. (*Digest,* 33.7.18.3)

Valerius Maximus records a story of a father travelling with his sick children to a river where he had been told they could be cured, who still took the time to heat the water before giving it to his thirsty children:

> wishing to succour them, since there was no fire on board [the ship], he learned from the skipper that smoke could be seen not far away … Eagerly he snatched up a cup and carried water drawn from the river to the place where the smoke had risen … The ground was smoking rather than bearing any remains of fire, so firmly seizing on the omen, he gathered some light fuel as chance supplied it, and blowing on it persistently, elicited a flame, heated the water, and gave it to the children to drink. (*Memorable Sayings*, 2.4.5)

At Pompeii at least 62 bronze vessels identified as used for boiling water have been found. They have carrying handles, lids and very characteristic profiles, with the widest part of the body immediately under the rim. This creates a vessel that would have been very difficult to clean if anything other than water was heated in it (see fig. 7).

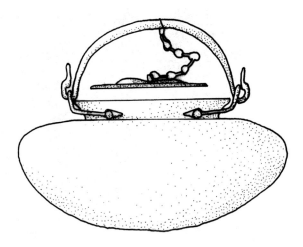

Fig. 7 Bronze vessel with lid, used for heating water, from Pompeii.

3

SUPPLY: COLLECTING FUEL

FIREWOOD

The fuel most commonly used on open fires and in ovens was wood (see figs 8, 9). Open fires were used for both cooking and heating, and to some extent lighting, in one-storey buildings in rural settlements, small towns and military establishments. Depending on the type of building, the hearth could be situated in the centre of the room, where the smoke had to find its own way out, or placed up against one wall, where occasionally chimneys took the smoke away. The fires would be banked up over night or during the day when not being used, but due to the difficulty of starting fires afresh they were often kept supplied with enough fuel to keep at least a spark alive. Large quantities of fuel were also required for houses with hypocausts. Once heated up to the correct temperature hypocausts could be fuel efficient, but there was an additional cost in terms of manpower as they needed to be regularly stoked.

Fig. 8 Man feeding firewood into an oven; relief from stone sarcophagus, Rome.

Fig. 9 Portable oven with firewood beside it, from mosaic showing kitchen implements in a villa at Marbella, Spain.

Sources of Firewood

The easiest way of collecting firewood was by picking up dead branches that had fallen to the forest floor. Varro explains the origins of the word for firewood (*lignum*) as coming from the word for 'to collect' (*legere*), 'because the wood that had fallen was gathered in the field to be used on the hearth' (*On the Latin Language*, 6.66). The wood was within easy reach of the collector, it was already dry and much of it was already of a suitable size for burning without the need for much cutting. It could be gathered at no cost from people's own land or from any forest considered to be a common resource that anyone was free to exploit. In historical times, some rich landowners would allow the poor to collect the fallen wood from their forests, but others saw it as a resource to be exploited for their own needs or profit, and no doubt it was similar in the Roman world. The drawback of this method of collecting fuel is that the sources become depleted by a heavy demand, and people have to walk further to find their fuel and spend more time gathering it.

A second way of acquiring firewood was to treat the woods as a crop and cut the trees themselves to provide the wood. Traditionally the product can be divided between 'timber', trees large enough to provide beams and planks, and 'wood', trees of a smaller diameter suitable for poles, wattles and firewood (Rackham 1982, 203). The unwanted branches of the trees cut down for timber were also used to provide firewood. Most 'wood' was 'underwood', a term used to describe trees grown especially for the purpose, usually by coppicing. In a managed wood most of the trees would be cut down young as underwood, while scattered through them were other trees that were allowed to grow large enough to provide timber. In the medieval period coppice rotations varied from four to nine years (Rackham 1982, 204; Galloway *et al.* 1996, 454). By 1086, only 15 per cent of England was woodland, and there may not have been much more in the Roman period. Little is known about Roman woodmanship, but with limited resources and a huge demand for both timber and wood, there is a good chance that in provinces with low levels of natural forest cover, woods were managed to maintain supplies (Rackham 1982, 200, 206). A legal discussion on what constituted 'firewood' for the purposes of legacies refers to a situation when a copse of wood had been marked out for cutting down for firewood; it was decided that only those trees already felled and lying on the ground ready to be cut up would be counted as 'firewood', while the still-standing timber was not (*Digest*, 32.56).

This second method of providing fuel required the fuel collector to own woodland or have access to common land, and also required more effort chopping, trimming and cutting, as well as having the resources to store it to dry before it was suitable for use. Green wood makes a very poor fuel since, depending on the type of wood and the time of year, it can be up to 50 per cent water. It is more difficult to light and when lit produces much less heat than dry wood. Burning green wood had other disadvantages, as experienced by some Roman travellers stopping at a villa, where smoke from the fire 'brought forth tears, as green wood, leaves and all, was burning on the brazier' (Horace, *Satires*, 1.5.80).

Different types of wood burn in different ways and give off a varying amount of heat, while some produce more smoke than others and some are worse for spitting out embers. Those who had a choice would go for those woods they knew were best, mainly hardwoods, but the poor would have had to take whatever they could find (Davidson 1986, 79). A study of charcoal from the furnace of a villa bath suite at Groundwell Ridge, Wiltshire, revealed that oak made up 78 per cent of the wood used as fuel, and that it might have been deliberately chosen as it is one of the best woods for producing sustained heat at a high temperature (McParland *et al.* 2009, 182).

Getting the Firewood

Collecting wood could be a very time-consuming task, especially if there was any distance to travel to get the wood. In modern Nepal a household spends an average of 41 hours per month collecting wood, the amount of time spent varying in the sample from 50 to 31 hours depending on the scarcity of the wood and the demand for it (Loughran and Pritchett 1997, section 2). The wood was not collected daily, and more than one member of the household would collect it at the same time, but this is still the equivalent of over an hour a day expended gathering fuel. Like water collecting, it was not a chore that could be overlooked as without it there was no way to cook meals. Firewood is not a particularly easy commodity to carry, being both heavy and awkwardly shaped. To make it easier to handle, it was usually tied into bundles (Varro mentions rushes used for tying: *On the Latin Language*, 5.31.137).

Traditionally firewood has been carried on the back (Davidson 1986, 79, fig. 49), which limits how much could be collected at any one time and creates the need for multiple trips. Those with the resources used pack animals when they could. They were used by the military on campaign (Livy, *History of Rome*, 41.1.7) and a slave collecting firewood for a villa used a donkey in Apuleius' novel *Metamorphoses*. It is not clear if the wood he was gathering was for the use of the estate or was to be sold as a crop, but the slave, a young lad, took the donkey out on a daily basis to collect firewood from a nearby mountain, using an axe to cut down the wood. He overloaded the donkey as much as he could get away with and was not averse to selling the firewood to people living nearby to make a bit of money on the side (*Metamorphoses*, 17–30).

Rural Settlements and Villas

In the countryside, firewood could be collected from convenient woods. In small settlements there would be little pressure for fuel, as long as there were woods nearby, and villa estates would include woods as part of their landholdings. When Martial woke up one morning during a visit to his villa he remarked that 'the hearth has a proud pile of firewood taken from a nearby grove of holm-oaks, and has been crowned by the farm-manager's wife with many a pot' (*Epigrams*, 12.19–21), while at Pliny's Laurentine villa 'the woods close by provide plenty of firewood and the town of Ostia supplies us with everything else' (*Letters*, 2.17.26). Firewood was considered a product of a country property in the same way as crops, as indicated in Roman law books which discussed people having the 'use' of a property without actually owning it:

> He may use firewood for his everyday needs and he may make use of the garden and take fruit, vegetables, flowers and water; however he may not do so, not so as to make a profit … it is worth considering whether he can use [the fruit, vegetables and firewood] only on the spot or whether they can also be brought into a town to him. (*Digest*, 7.8.12)

Military

The Roman army, whether on the move or settled in permanent establishments, required a huge quantity of firewood. When the army was on campaign, its supply could become a major problem for the army commanders. Vegetius observed that one of the duties of a camp prefect was to make sure there was no shortage of firewood and that on campaign 'problems of firewood and fodder in winter, and of water in summer should be avoided' (*Epitome of Military Science*, 2.10, 3.3). During campaigns it was the soldiers themselves who had to collect wood. When the legions in Pannonia mutinied in the first century AD, they listed some of their grievances to Germanicus who had come to deal with the situation: 'they taunted him with the fees [they had to pay] for exemptions from duty, the miserly rates of pay, and the severity of the work; the rampart-building, the digging of the defensive ditches, and the collection of forage, building materials and firewood were specifically mentioned' (Tacitus, *Annals*, 1.35). It was a particularly dangerous occupation when the enemy were close, as the wood gatherers (like water collectors) were very vulnerable to attack. In the war against the Histrians in 178 BC Livy records that units of soldiers were given the duty of protecting those outside the camp, the water collectors and those looking for firewood and forage (*History of Rome*, 41.1.7). At other times such soldiers seemed to have had little or no protection. In 208 BC Numidians waited outside the Roman camp 'in case they might be able to capture any men, who in wandering about in search of fodder or firewood, had gone too far from camp' and again in 212 BC Masinissa 'captured soldiers who had wandered far from the camp in search of wood and fodder' (*ibid.*, 25.34.4, 27.27.3).

In such cases, the author makes the point that the men had to go some distance to find sufficient wood, which is not surprising when considering the need to find enough dry wood for tens of thousands of men on a daily basis. Caesar took advantage of this during the civil wars, when his opponent took up a position in a reoccupied camp: 'Of his soldiers who were free from work owing to the fortifications being intact, some were going to a distance for the purpose of getting firewood and fodder', while others returned to their previous camp for the baggage they had left behind. Caesar unexpectedly moved his army, but Pompey was unable to follow because of his dispersed troops (Caesar, *Civil Wars*, 3.76).

The arrangement for supplying units with firewood when in their permanent bases is not so clear. It is possible the army had control over their own managed woodlands so that they could ensure a steady supply of suitable dried wood, and sent soldiers with pack animals or carts on a regular basis to bring it into camp for distribution. Alternately they may have bought in their firewood along with all the other supplies they needed. The only known military 'firewood agent' (*agentium in lignariis*) is one connected to a vexillation of the 21st Legion in Germany in the early third century (*CIL* 13.6618, 6623 and 11781).

A writing tablet from Vindolanda recording sums of money received from some people and the amount owed by others has the entry 'For firewood purchased, 7[+] *denarii*', but it is not clear if this was part of the unit administration or a private transaction (Bowman 1994, 111). It may be that some soldiers bought (or collected) extra firewood for their own use (perhaps because they felt the official allocation was not sufficient). The soldiers, however, may have avoided doing much of the hard work of gathering the wood themselves: the second-century grammarian Festus gave one definition of the word *calo* as 'slaves of the soldiers, so-called because they carry loads of firewood which the Greeks call *kala*' (Roth 1999, 102).

A letter from Vindolanda addressed to one Cassius Saecularis, known to have been involved in supplying barley to the fort, also mentions firewood: '... they will have the authority of Severinus. For I have got [it?] from him, if any-one wants to come, and he will not mind where they are storing the firewood and building timbers'

(Birley 2002, 91). A daily report of the Twentieth Cohort of Palmyrenes found at Dura-Europos records a soldier called Zebidas being sent out 'as wood-gatherer for the baths', although as a single soldier would not be able to supply enough wood for a bathhouse, it may be that he was going to collect a load rather than gather it himself (Fink 1971, 47, column ii, line 9). Collecting wood was a distinctly low-status occupation. When Maecenas was discussing soldiers being allowed to enter the senate, he made the proviso 'except such as have served in the rank and file. For it is both a shame and a reproach that men of this sort, who have carried faggots and charcoal, should be found on the roll of the senate' (Dio Cassius, *Roman History*, 52.25.7).

Towns and Cities

In small towns, the distance to areas suitable for wood-collecting that were not under the control of landowners, and the numbers of people trying to make use of the same resources, would have meant collecting fuel for free would be difficult, and in cities it would have been impossible. It has been estimated that wood from the equivalent of 10,000km^2 would be needed to keep a city of 100,000 supplied with firewood for heating needs over a year (Bairoch 1988, 14). Occupants of towns and cities therefore had little choice but to buy their fuel from traders. Local farmers produced firewood or charcoal as a crop and sold it either directly to town dwellers or, probably more frequently, to professional wood sellers who would collect the wood at source using carts or pack animals (Blyth 1999, 96). As firewood is bulky compared to its sale value, it was uneconomic to transport firewood very far: in the fourteenth century it has been estimated at no more than 22km (13.7 miles), although charcoal could be transported further as it had a higher value by weight (Galloway *et al.* 1996, 450, 454, 458). The poor people who had 'to buy their cabbage and firewood' (Juvenal, *Satires*, 1.134) were unable to afford large quantities and must have been forced to use it very sparingly. Comparison with later periods suggests they would have lit fires only when needed instead of keeping one burning constantly, and would have had fewer hot meals in their own home.

Diocletian's *Edict of Maximum Prices* includes a section on the cost of firewood in the fourth century, listed according to the method of transportation (14.8–12). The price is probably that paid for the wood at source, so that the cost of transportation to market would have been added before it was sold in town (Blyth 1999, 92):

Wagon load of wood	1200lb	150 *denarii*
Camel load of wood	400lb	50 *denarii*
Hinny load	300lb	30 *denarii*
Ass load	200lb	[20?] *denarii*
Chips or twigs for use in ovens	bundles of 15lb	30 *denarii*

The finer twigs were used to heat bread ovens, where a clay-lined, domed oven was heated up by burning wood inside it. The bread was put into the oven after the wood ash had been raked out of the heated oven (Croom 2001, 37). If 6.3kg of wood is taken as a possible daily requirement for the poor (see below), it would cost approximately 1.5 *denarii* to buy the firewood, less than the price of a pint of Egyptian beer or a shave (both 2 *denarii*).

Storing Firewood

In historical times it was common to collect enough fuel during the summer months to last throughout the winter. Whether it was one week's or a year's supply, or green wood being kept while it dried, the firewood would need to be stored somewhere dry. As nowadays, the bulk of the wood would be stored outside under some form of cover, being brought inside shortly before it was needed for a final drying. Cato recommended that chopped olive wood and roots should be made into conical ricks, and that firewood should be stored in the loft (*On Farming*, 55), and a poor countrywoman kept firewood in the roof space for her fire (Ovid, *Metamorphoses*, 8, 644). The wood may also have been stacked against buildings under the shelter of deep eaves or under specially built structures to keep the rain off. The quantities of wood being stored could be sizeable; in thirteenth-century London, streets could be obstructed by the large heaps of logs stored outside houses, and it may have been similar in Roman cities (Galloway *et al.* 1996, 452). Keeping the fire going would require constant trips outside by slaves or family members to replenish the fuel supply.

Quantities Required

When Vitruvius talks about the need to stockpile supplies in cities that are likely to be besieged, he observes that:

> in times of sieges, the provision of everything is easier than that of firewood … Water is obtained by the digging of wells; in sudden storms it is received from the sky from the roof tiles. But the provision of firewood, which is necessary for cooking food, is difficult and troublesome, for it takes time to collect and is used in large quantities. (*On Architecture*, 5.9.8–9)

The quantity of fuel required over a year could be quite substantial, although it is difficult to estimate just how much wood was required on a daily basis. The quantity would also vary across the empire and throughout the year, depending on whether the fuel was required just for cooking or also for heating. Heating could involve either simple open fires or more complex under-floor heating systems which required a much larger quantity of fuel. In addition they also required a slave who was available to keep the fire stoked both day and night. Hypocausts were used in high–status houses, heating a number of the more important rooms as well as a small bath suite, but were also widespread in quite modest buildings which had only one or two heated rooms. A large quantity of fuel was required to get the system up to temperature, but needed much less fuel to maintain the heat. A modern experiment has shown that 1kg of charcoal per hour is needed to keep a single room of 20m² at a temperature of 20°C (Rook 1978, 277). Calculations for the free-standing bathhouse at Welwyn suggest 114 tonnes of fuel was needed per year; modern public *hammams* in Morocco use an average of 179 tonnes per year (*ibid.*, 281; Wauthelet 1998, table 1: *hammams* traditionally use wood chips, twigs, domestic rubbish and olive kernels as fuel rather than large pieces of wood).

In nineteenth-century Cornwall, where furze was used as fuel, it was estimated that 1000 faggots (made up of four smaller bundles, each of which was an armful of furze) were needed for the winter supply of a farm (Davidson 1986, 76). In late eighteenth-century Philadelphia, accounts record that four journeyman silversmiths used an average of 4.88 cords of wood per year, while the rich were said to get through 25 cords (Smith 1993, 150). A cord is a traditional measurement for firewood, consisting of a pile 8ft long by 4ft wide and 4ft high. The quantity of wood involved would depend on the type of timber used, whether it was green or dry, and how well it was stacked. Modern estimates for the weight of a cord vary between about 2 to 4.5 tonnes, so the journeymen were using at least 9.76 tonnes of wood per year, which equates to 26.7kg per day.

Table 2: Quantities of Firewood used on a Daily Basis

Area	Source	Daily (kg)
Raipur, India, for cooking only	Dunkerley *et al.* 1990, 93	2.6
Pre-industrial Europe combined, low estimate	Bairoch 1988, 14	2.7
Pre-industrial Europe combined, high estimate	Bairoch 1988, 14	4.4
Pre-industrial northern Europe, low estimate	Bairoch 1988, 14	4.4
Post-medieval London	Galloway *et al.* 1996, 455	4.9
Pre-industrial northern Europe, high estimate	Bairoch 1988, 14	6.3
Kenya	World Agroforest Centre	6.8
Ghana and Burkina	GLOWA Volta project	16.9
Philadelphia 1770s, low estimate	Smith 1993, 150	26.7
Philadelphia 1770s, high estimate	Smith 1993, 150	63.0
Philadelphia, the rich, low estimate	Smith 1993, 150	137.0

Table 2 shows a range of figures for firewood consumption from a number of different periods and locations. It can be seen from the wide variations that it is impossible to estimate a 'typical' amount of wood used by a Roman. A poor person, with one household fire used for both cooking and heating, would use only a fraction of that used by a family with a separate kitchen that needed fuel for cooking and other rooms that required fuel for heating, let alone a rich person with a multi-roomed house, a bath suite and rooms with under-floor heating, as well as large numbers of slaves to be fed and watered.

Plate 3 shows approximately 2.7kg of firewood, which is the low estimate for firewood requirements for pre-industrial Europe. A quick, unscientific experiment by the re-enactment group *Cohors V Gallorum* showed that this was enough to fuel a fire for only one hour. The wood was seasoned and dry, and made up of branches about 20mm in diameter. It was added to an established fire and used to heat 2 litres of water in a replica coarse-ware cooking pot placed in the centre of the hearth. The water took 20 minutes to boil, and it remained hot for 40 minutes, by which time the original wood was all reduced to ash.

The necessity for heating drinking water, baking bread and cooking meals as well as heating the room and banking up the fire indicates that most Romans would have used much more than 2.7kg of wood per day. A likely exception would be the urban poor who had to buy their fuel and presumably used as little as possible, not boiling drinking water and buying bread or cooking their own in a baker's oven for a small fee. A single mixed infantry and cavalry fort of about 600 men using 6.3kg of wood per day (the high estimate for pre-medieval northern Europe) per *contubernium* or officer's house would use two-thirds of a tonne of wood every day, without taking into account the requirements of the commanding officer's house with its private bath suite and the large external bathhouse for the troops.

OTHER FUELS

In modern times, 'firewood' usually means large chunks of wood taken from mature trees, but in historical times people have burnt a large range of material in an effort to keep warm, the poor in particular making use of anything they could collect for free. This has included dung, hedgerow twigs, furze, gorse, heather, dried seaweed, straw, stubble and weeds, as well as wood, peat and coal (Davidson 1986, 73–6). It is clear that in the Roman period a similar approach was taken to sourcing fuel. The legal definition of firewood in the *Digest of Justinian* includes wood from felled trees along with:

> twigs, charcoal and olive stones, which are good only for burning, and also acorns and other kernels … If the testator's wishes are not against it, twigs, brushwood, prunings, chips from timber and the stems and roots of vines will be included. In

certain regions such as Egypt, where reeds are used instead of firewood, the term
'firewood' will include reeds and papyrus plants and certain kinds of grasses and
thorns or briars ... In certain provinces they use cow–dung for this purpose ...
Whole pinecones will be included under the term 'firewood'. (32.56)

Pliny also mentions that the outer skin of the flax plant was used 'for heating ovens
and furnaces' (*Natural Histories*, 19.2.18). Documents from Egypt also record straw
being used to fuel a furnace during construction work and chaff used to fire a pottery
kiln (Parsons 2007, 86, 114).

Charcoal

If there was no market for firewood, Cato recommended making charcoal instead
(*On Farming*, 38.4). Although it used up large quantities of wood in its production,
charcoal could be transported further than firewood and still make a profit, and could
be sold for more per weight. Despite its expense, it was often preferred as a fuel, as
it tended to burn with less smoke and at a higher temperature. It was used for both
heating and cooking, although not always at the same time.

Whilst firewood could be used for open fires in one-storey buildings, the general
lack of chimney flues to get rid of the smoke meant that such fires could not be
used in multiple-floor buildings, so other heating methods were required. Under-
floor heating could be used by the well-off, but a more flexible method of heating
rooms was by burning charcoal in portable braziers. Suetonius mentions braziers used
to warm dining rooms (one unfortunately setting alight to the room), while Cicero
recommends a glowing brazier to a soldier settled in winter quarters, especially since
he knew he did not have many thick cloaks to keep him warm (Suetonius, *Twelve
Caesars*, Vitellius, 8.2; Tiberius, 74; Cicero, *Letters*, 7.10.2).

Examples of braziers from Pompeii have a decorated circular or rectangular outer casing
of bronze and an inner cage of iron to hold the charcoal (dell'Orto and Varone 1992, no 58;
Adam 2005, fig. 621). If the iron tray was removable it made cleaning out the ashes easier;
with some post-Roman examples it also meant the tray could be swapped, morning and
evening, with one already full of fuel. More recent parallels also suggest that the charcoal
was often set on top of a layer of insulating ashes to avoid the outer metal container
growing too hot, or with ashes placed over the top to stop the fuel burning too quickly.

Although burning charcoal inside is not now recommended because it produces
carbon monoxide, it has a long history as a method of heating rooms in many cultures.
Sometimes the braziers were freestanding and could be moved to be close to the
person wanting to be warm, and sometimes they were placed in a fixed position,
often in the centre of the room or under a table, as in Iran where the traditional form
of heating was the *korsi*, 'a low table covered with blankets and quilts under which a

charcoal brazier burnt slowly, its embers covered with a thick layer of ashes to ensure an even distribution of heat and prevent burning'. People sat round it with hands and feet under the blankets and used the top as a table for meals (Guppy 1989, 96).

As with an open hearth, there were drawbacks to this method of heating. In 1671 a Chinese dramatist complained about the cost of using multiple braziers to heat his study and the fact that it resulted in a fine layer of ashes over his desk (Handler 2001, 326), while a British medical officer in Lisbon in 1812 observed:

> As the houses seem constructed entirely to alleviate the effects of heat, they are not calculated to reserve the inhabitants from cold, and, as a substitute for a grate, a small iron vase is used into which charcoal is put previously burnt to a red heat to dissipate the noxious fumes: but the unpleasant, and certainly unwholesome effect, which this mode of warming a room produced, frequently counterbalances the advantage derived from its heat. (Broughton 2005, 23)

In the Roman period the author Lucretius also refers to 'the strong heavy fumes of charcoal creeping into the brain, unless we have taken water beforehand' (*On the Nature of Things*, 6.802), and at least one emperor died of carbon monoxide poisoning. The Emperor Julian had not ordered the hypocaust to be lit in the house where he was staying as he thought the winter was mild enough, but when the temperature fell one night he ordered a brazier brought into his room. After feeling ill, he was taken outside and recovered, but his successor was not so lucky; Emperor Jovian had a brazier in his tent one night during a harsh winter, but falling asleep after a heavy meal and wine, he was not in a position to realise anything was wrong and died during the night (Lascaratos and Marketos 1998, 103–4). In both cases it was thought that the steam coming from damp walls was to blame rather than fumes from the fuel (*ibid.*, 106). Carbon monoxide gas is produced as the result of the incomplete burning of carbon-based fuels, and is colourless, odourless and tasteless. It is highly toxic in poorly ventilated rooms, but it is likely that usually most Roman rooms were draughty enough for charcoal to be used safely.

Many households would have used both firewood and charcoal in different parts of the house, and a discussion of what should be included under the term 'stores' (which referred to food for use by the owner, not that for sale), queried whether the 'logs [and] charcoal' used to prepare the food that made up the 'stores' should also be included (*Digest*, 33.9.3.9). Charcoal was particularly used for cooking in larger houses which had separate kitchens containing raised cooking hearths. These were masonry raised platforms built against a wall about 0.6m to 1m high, ranging in size (in one survey of Pompeian examples) from 0.75m to 3.25m long and 0.5m to 1.45m wide (Allison 2004, 99; fig. 5.11). There was a slight raised lip round the top, but otherwise the whole upper surface could be covered with charcoal and used for cooking, with

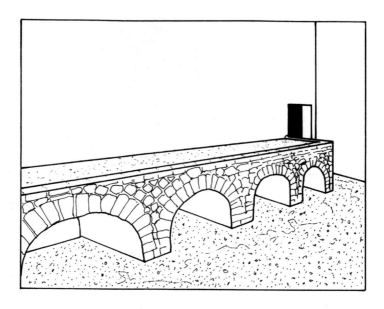

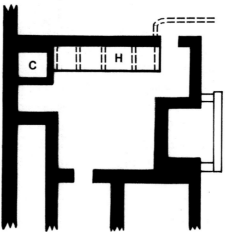

Fig. 10 The kitchen in the Villa S. Marco, Stabia. Top: view showing cooking platform with storage alcoves underneath. Bottom: plan of the kitchen showing cooking platform (H) and large water cistern (C).

space for numerous pots or grills to be used at the same time. Very often the front of the cooking hearth had a large arched recess in it that may have been used for the storage of cooking vessels or of fuel for immediate use, taken from a larger indoor store somewhere else in the house (see fig. 10). Collecting charcoal from the store would have been a dirtier business than collecting firewood, and must have required the use of a bucket or sack or similar.

Dung

Despite the smell produced by burning cow or horse dung, it was often a popular fuel for the rural poor in historical times, since it was easy to collect, it was usually in plentiful supply and it burnt well, having a higher calorific value than wood (Davidson 1986, 77). The dung was collected from the fields, usually left on walls to dry, and then stored under cover. It is not known how commonly it was used in the Roman period, since it could also be used as manure for crops, but it was certainly known as a fuel. Livy describes an area in Galatia 'which is called Axylon [= "woodless"]. It derives its name from the fact that it not only produces no wood at all but not even thorns or any other wood for fire; they used cow-dung in place of fire-wood' (*History of Rome*, 38.18). Isidore also describes the origin of the word 'fire-shovel' (*rutabulum*), 'so called from tossing dung, or fire, for the sake of cooking bread' (Isidore, *Etymologies*, 20.8.6, trans. Barney *et al.* 2006), and in Egypt, merchants selling dung were among those who had to pay market taxes (Parsons 2007, 104).

Coal

In the Roman period coal was collected from exposed seams on the surface or through river and coastal erosion rather than by sub-surface mining. Evidence for its use has been found in France, Germany and Britain, and although it was probably used mainly for metal-working, it has also been found in some domestic situations. Traces of coal have been discovered in a number of hearths and possible bread ovens, but especially in hypocausts in villas, military camps and bathhouses (Dearne and Brannigan 1995, 75, 82–3). Coal really needs to be burnt in a raised grate with a closed chimney to draw the noxious smoke away, and was unsuitable for use in open hearths with only a smoke hole in the roof (Davidson 1986, 92). Different coals also had different burning qualities, with some being very difficult to light, some fusing together and having to be regularly broken with a poker to stop the fire going out, and others producing large quantities of ash (*ibid.*, 93). It was also very dirty compared to other fuels: it was messy to carry through the house to the fire and chimneys required regular cleaning, which unavoidably left soot in the room afterwards (*ibid.*, 95). In the Roman period there was no clear advantage to using coal over wood and it never became a major fuel source in domestic situations, apart perhaps from hypocausts where the drawbacks to coal use would not have been so obvious.

Peat

This was not a fuel used in the Mediterranean region due to the lack of peat bogs, but it was used in various countries before the Roman occupation and no doubt continued to be used afterwards. Pliny records a tribe called the Chauci who were said to live in a region without trees (the north-west coast of modern Germany) digging up this 'mud', as he called it, drying it and burning it to cook with (*Natural Histories*, 16.1.4). Peat has been found during excavations at both Carlisle and York; the quantities of peat found at York suggest it was in common use there, although it cannot be proved it was used for fuel rather than for any other purpose, such as animal bedding (Hall *et al.* 1990, 413).

In historical times it usually took between two and four days to cut a year's supply of peat, although the drying and transport took longer. It has to be cut out of the ground in blocks, laid out in a field to dry for about a week, stacked up and dried further for another couple of weeks, and then transported back to the house to be re-stacked ready for use. In areas of Ireland where peat was easily available, a family would use up to 40 tonnes of peat a year (Davidson 1986, 83, 86). Peat fires were easy to lay, required less attention than wood fires and burnt very cleanly.

LIGHTING FIRES

Lighting a fire required creating a spark to set light to very dry, very light material (tinder) that would burn easily and quickly. This would then be placed in the midst of thin slivers of wood or other material (kindling) that would then catch light, over which could be placed the thicker, true firewood. Pliny records that the skill of lighting fires from flints was invented by one Pyrodes, son of Cilix (*Natural Histories*, 7.56.199), while the army on the move made use of stones such as iron pyrites and another stone that is possibly flint or emery: 'stones known as "live stones" are extremely heavy and are indispensable to reconnaissance parties preparing a camp-site. When struck with a nail or another stone they give off a spark, and if this is caught on sulphur or else on dry fungi or leaves it produces a flame instantaneously' (Pliny, *Natural Histories*, 36.30.138). Pyrites were also used by 'common people [who] call this the "hearth rock"', and was notable because it 'starts a fire quicker than one can speak' (Isidore, *Etymologies*, 16.4.5; trans. Barney *et al.* 2006). Isidore also mentions that 'when crystal is placed facing the sun's rays it seizes the flame so that it sets fire to dried fungus or leaves', but it is not clear if this was a common way of lighting fires or merely a party piece (*ibid.*, 16.13.1).

Fire sticks could also be used:

> this has been discovered by experience in the camps of military scouting parties and of shepherds, because there is not always a stone at hand to strike fire with; consequently two pieces of wood are rubbed together and catch fire owing to the friction, and the fire is caught in a lump of dry tinder, fungus or dead leaves catching most readily. (Pliny, *Natural Histories*, 16.77.208)

A number of woods could be used for making fire sticks, including mulberry, laurel and ivy, which were all classified as 'hot' woods. 'There is nothing better than ivy wood for rubbing against and laurel wood for rubbing with; one of the wild vines ... which climbs up a tree like ivy, is also spoken well of' (*ibid.*, 16.76.207–16.77.209). Tinder could be sulphur, leaves, wood or dried fungi. In *Etymologies*, Isidore describes tinder as 'splinters that are cast off from trees by lopping, or charred shavings, or hollowed-out firewood. It takes its name from 'dried fungus' because they catch fire in the same way' (17.6.26; 17.10.18, trans. Barney *et al.* 2006).

Since lighting fires from scratch could be a long and frustrating process, it was much easier to keep a fire burning during the day and banked up when it was not required (in particular overnight) so that there was always an ember to restart the fire. A poem about a farmer preparing breakfast describes how he lit a lamp from the fire, as 'a tiny stream of smoke still lingered from a burnt-out log, while ashes concealed the gleam of buried coals' (Anonymous, *Moretum*, 8–9). It is possible the fire was also banked up during the day when it was not needed for cooking. Ovid describes an old woman in Italy preparing a meal for guests, which would suggest it was at least mid-afternoon if not later:

> She raked aside the warm ashes on the hearth and fanned yesterday's coals to life, which she fed with leaves and dry bark, blowing them into flame with the breath of her old body. Then she took down from the roof some fine-split wood and dry twigs, broke them up and placed them under the little copper pan. (*Metamorphoses*, 8.641–5)

Even if a fire went out, there was usually a neighbour who would provide a few glowing embers, avoiding the need to light it from scratch. In one study in modern Africa, it was noted that there was no concern if the fire should go out as it was unlikely that all the fires in the village would go out at the same time, and another house could easily supply some embers (Reynolds 1964, 76); there is some suggestion that the same attitude existed in the Roman world. When Aesop's master ordered dinner earlier than usual there was no fire lit in the kitchen and Aesop had to go 'around to several houses in search of fire and at last found a place to light his lamp' (Phaedrus, *Fables*, 3.19.1–3).

An easy way of collecting the embers was to carry them on a sherd of broken pottery, although Pliny also mentions an ancient method of carrying fire in a hollow fennel stalk (Ovid, *Calendar*, 11.638; Pliny, *Natural Histories*, 7.56.199). In the novel *Satyricon*, Petronius describes a fire being lit after having been accidentally extinguished:

> [Oenothea] ran off to her neighbours to see to reviving the fire ... I had not yet got outside the small house when I saw Oenothea coming with a sherd full of

live coals … She made up a fire raised out of some dead reeds, and after heaping on a quantity of fire-wood, proceeded to apologize for her delay, saying that her friend would not let her go until the customary three cups had been emptied. (136)

Kindling

The wood of the stone pine (called 'torch pine' by the Romans since it was commonly used for torches) and wood chips were used as kindling (Pliny, *Natural Histories*, 16.18.44; Ovid, *Metamorphoses*, 8.460), while Cato suggests a suitable winter task for farm slaves was making faggots of wood pruned from vines and trees, and fig wood for kindling for the 'owners' use', and a country-woman 'built a fire with dried reeds' before adding wood on top (*On Farming*, 37.5; 50; Petronius, *Satyricon*, 136). The kindling was sometimes 'improved' to make it burn better. Cato instructed: 'drench chopped olive wood and other firewood with raw *amurca* [lees of olive oil] and place in the sun. Let it soak in well. After this they will not be smoky and will burn well' (Cato, *On Farming*, 130).

Ovid observed that 'a cinder nearly spent will live, if you touch it with sulphur, and from a small fire become a mighty one' (*Remedies of Love*, 731), and kindling sticks were also dipped in sulphur. There are a number of references to street traders bartering 'yellow sulphur matches' for broken glass, which they could sell on for a better price (Martial, *Epigrams*, 1.41.3–5, 10.3.3; Juvenal, *Satires*, 5.48; cf. 13.145). These were not like modern matches which act as the source of fire, but had to be lit from some other source. The sticks may have been lit from the tinder and used to light the kindling before being blown out to be saved for later re-use, as with more modern 'brimstone matches' (Davidson 1986, 96), or they may have been one-use kindling like the oil-soaked wood (see plate 4).

4

SUPPLY: GRINDING

Plautus' list of activities for a female slave in *The Merchant* (see above, p. 10) includes grinding wheat to produce flour. The same list also includes producing woollen thread, repeated in a fragment of Lucilius: 'let her chop wood, spin her weight of wool, sweep the rooms and take a hiding' (*Satires*, 27.747). Although not housework in the modern sense, they were daily activities in a Roman household and in literature at least seen to be on a par with other aspects of housework.

GRINDING WHEAT

The most common type of grain used for human consumption in the Roman period was wheat. There were three main types in use: emmer, which produced a heavy bread but good quality porridges and cakes; spelt, which was better for bread, and bread wheat, also good (as its name suggests) for bread, with the added advantage that it required less initial preparation than spelt (Cool 2006, 70). An account from the fort at Vindolanda lists a variety of wheat types, suggesting that the differences in the grain were understood and deliberately used (*ibid.*, 70). A further choice could be made of different grades of flour, according to how many times the grain was ground and sieved, and how much bran was removed.

Cereal grain consists of the germ, the starchy bulk and bran, the hard outer cover. Bran can make up to about 23 per cent of the grain being ground, and since it is inedible for humans it was generally removed for use as animal feed. Once ground, the grain could be divided between good quality flour, 'second-rate' flour and bran. Poor people used most of the grain, retaining the inedible bran to give more bulk to the flour, creating flour 'considerably darker than wholemeal' (Moritz 1958, 212). *Farina*, the grade of flour produced in domestic settings for non-commercial baking, was also probably made up of most of the grain, perhaps with about 10 per cent discarded as bran, and would have been similar to modern wholemeal. In wealthy houses the finest flour (only 25 per cent of the original grain weight) would be separated out for the rich to make soft white bread while the rest was left for use by the rest of the household.

Processes

The grain had first to be cleaned of the chaff (the dry outer protective casings) that had not already been removed by threshing and winnowing, as well as any other unwanted material such as weed seeds. Some pieces could be removed by sieving, but seeds and other fragments of a similar size to the grain itself had to be picked out by hand. This would have been a tedious but necessary task, since the seeds of the corn cockle, a common crop contaminant, could cause abdominal pains, vomiting, diarrhoea and dizziness if eaten. The wheat was then ground using a rotary stone quern. Oils in the bran and germ oxidise on being milled and turn rancid, meaning that the flour could not be stored as long as the whole grain, so it is likely the grinding was done on a regular basis as required rather than large quantities of flour being produced and then stockpiled.

　　The quern was usually set on the ground; post-Roman parallels suggest having a cloth or skin or sometimes a wooden box under it to catch the flour was typical although not universal, and a number of Roman lower quern stones have been found set into the floor rather than just sitting on it (Cool 2007, 74). At some sites in Britain querns seem to have been set on slightly raised platforms. At Vindolanda the lower

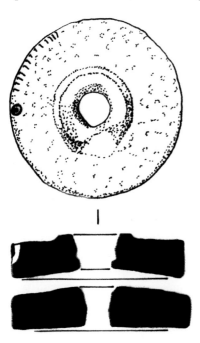

stone of a quern was found set into a raised bench two stone courses high, its grinding surface projecting 1–2cm above the bench top (see fig. 11; Bidwell 1985, fig. 29). This is a rare example of a complete quern surviving from the Roman period, as the matching upper stone was found reused in the floor of the next period (*ibid.*, 68). The position of the quern would have meant some of the flour would have fallen on to the floor as well as on to the bench.

Fig. 11 Quern from Vindolanda Roman fort. Top: upper stone. Bottom: cross-section of upper and lower stones. (After Bidwell 1985)

In Scotland in the eighteenth and nineteenth centuries, and in other cultures up until the twentieth century, it was usual for two women to work together, either both turning the handle together or else taking it in turns to rotate the stone, pour in the grain and collect the flour, while often singing at the same time to make the time pass (cf. Pennant 1774, pl. XXXIV and the painting *The hand mill* by R.R. McIan, 1847). That this method was also used in Palestine in Roman times is indicated by Jesus' comment that 'two women will be grinding at the mill; one is taken and one is left' (Matthew 24:41).

Grinding the grain only once would have produced a coarse flour. It is likely that the ground grain was usually sieved and the larger fragments ground a second time (Moritz 1958, 178). The resulting flour could then be sieved again to remove the bran and any surviving large fragments, which could then be re-ground if necessary.

Table 3: Time Taken to Grind Grain by One Person, Standardised to Kilograms per Hour

Location	kg/hr	
Surkhet, Nepal (max.)	10.0	Shrestha undated, table 1
Surkhet, Nepal (min.)	8.0	Shrestha undated, table 1
Baitadi, Nepal (max.)	5.0	Shrestha undated, table 1
Baitadi, Nepal (min.)	4.0	Shrestha undated, table 1
Scotland	3.6	Jasny 1950, 241
Algeria	2.0	Cool 2006, 73
India	1.8	Cool 2006, 73

Table 3 shows that the time taken to produce flour in more recent times can vary considerably; the quality of the quern and the number of times the grain was ground would also affect how long it took. It has been estimated a Roman soldier was given approximately 850g of wheat per day (if made into bread, this would give him roughly 65 per cent of the suggested 3000 calories required by a soldier: Roth 1999, 48), which it would take him at the most half an hour to convert into flour. Matters would grow more complicated if all eight soldiers in the *contubernium* wanted to grind their daily grain allowance; whether each soldier ground their own or one soldier took it in turns to grind the lot, it would take four hours every day to produce flour for the whole *contubernium*. Having at least some of their ration given to them as flour produced in military watermills would have saved the soldiers a lot of time.

Farms and Small Settlements

One of Plutarch's *Roman Questions* asked: 'Why in the early days did they not allow their wives to grind grain or to cook?', with the answer explaining that 'when they had carried off the Sabines' daughters and later, after warring with the Sabines, had had peace, it was specified among the other articles of agreement that no Sabine woman should grind grain for a Roman or cook for him' (*Moralia, Roman Questions*, 85). The tasks were presumably given to slaves to do instead, but the fact that the special dispensation was made shows it was not unusual for Roman wives to do the grinding. Nor was the job always given to low-caste slaves: Cato advised that the wife of the farm manager 'must be able to make good flour and emmer-wheat groats' (*On Farming*, 143).

Grinding wheat was not a task carried out only by women. An early Roman poem records a male farmer getting up to grind the wheat for a loaf of bread before he wakes his female slave to put fuel on the fire and heat up some water. He first cleaned the quern with a brush and then ground 16lb (*c*.5.2kg) of grain, feeding it in with one hand and turning the upper stone with the other, singing to himself to pass the time (Anonymous, *Moretum*). If the quantity ground is not just poetic licence, he was producing enough flour for approximately six people at the ration rate of a soldier or, if there was only himself and his female slave in his household, enough flour for the two of them for three days. When he had ground the flour he sieved it to remove the bran and larger fragments and made a loaf of bread with the warmed water.

Cato's list of requirements for a 60-hectare olive farm includes one donkey mill, one pushing mill, one Spanish mill and a mortar plus pestle to pound emmer wheat (*On Farming*, 10). The designs for the pushing and Spanish mills are not clear, but the three types must have had different functions involving either the material to be ground or the nature of the finished product.

Military Establishments

As there were no mess halls or central food preparation in military establishments, all soldiers had to prepare and cook their own food within their individual sub-units (*contubernia*). The wheat that was given as part of the ration was stored as grain, so the soldiers had to clean and grind it themselves. At South Shields fort the study of a granary destroyed by fire revealed more cleaning debris close to the entrance than in the body of the building, suggestive of soldiers collecting their allocation and cleaning it in the better light by the door, although it is not clear why they should do it here rather than back in their own barracks (van der Veen 1994, 256). Fragments of querns are common finds in Roman sites, although it is not known how many shared use of an individual quern. A few inscribed querns have been found, most of which refer to them being the property of the century, although one from the Saalburg in Germany mentions the name of the *contubernium* (Frere and Tomlin 1992, 94). From the length of time it took to grind flour, it seems likely each *contubernium* had access to a quern.

However, at a number of forts, there were associated watermills that could have produced large quantities of flour for the garrison at a fraction of the time required for hand-turned querns. A leat for a watermill inserted through the base of a tower and ramp connected to the road bridge at Chesters suggest that the watermill was part of the official infrastructure (Bidwell 2007, 83). Watermills are also known from near Birdoswald and Greatchesters forts, and it is probable that there were originally many more, some of which have remained undiscovered since they are not in the immediate vicinity of the fort itself, and others which may have been washed away (Spain 2002, 55).

Large Towns and Urban Settlements

In larger towns cereal processing was not done on a household basis. A study of selected rubbish pits at Pompeii showed that chaff was associated with cereal remains in rubbish deposits dating from the fourth to the first half of the second century BC, indicating household processing, but was absent from deposits of later date, suggesting it was then being carried out on rural villa sites or at the properties of professional bakers (Ciaraldi and Richardson 2000, 76).

In the Mediterranean region the grinding was carried out by bakers on a professional basis, using large slave- or animal-driven millstones. The most famous types were the massive hourglass stones driven by donkeys (Nappo 1998, fig. 75, 76–7; Apuleius, *Metamorphoses*, 9.11–3). It is usually stated that the bakers ground the flour for their own use, to make the bread they then sold, but some clearly also ground additional grain, as Pliny mentions the cost of flour, indicating it was available for purchase, and the accounts of a baker in Oxyrhynchus in Egypt lists measures of 'fine flour' supplied alongside large loaves, white bread loaves, crisp cakes and section cakes (Moritz 1958, 171; *Natural Histories*, 18.20.90; Parsons 2007, 109). Certainly in the late fourth century the *Edict of Dynamius* in Rome tried to stop millers from overcharging or giving short measures to their customers (Wilson 2003, 107).

Mills

Millstones were stones too large to be rotated by human power. At Rome a series of 12 worn-out millstones (from at least five different mills) reused as flooring had diameters between 0.83m and 0.97m, as compared to the average sizes of hand-turned querns of roughly 0.4m (*ibid.*, 88). The millstones could be powered by either animals or by water, but it appears that in many parts of the empire water-powered mills would have been much more common than animal-powered ones. In Britain, for example, several hundred disc millstones are known, but only a very few pieces of the hourglass donkey-powered millstones. Locally available stone was not suitable for this type of millstone, so any hourglass stone would have had to have been imported at some cost (Spain 2002, 54). The design of some disc millstones in Britain and Cyrenaica indicate they were overdriven, which implies they were driven by animals, but the great majority of millstones were under-driven and would have been powered by water (Wilson 2003, 87). Water-powered mills would have been more efficient in any case, having a greater speed; it is estimated a disc millstone would produce approximately six times as much flour as an hourglass millstone of the same diameter (*ibid.*, 54). Calculations produced for a study of the military watermill on Haltwhistle Burn near Greatchesters fort suggest it could have produced approximately 58kg per hour (*ibid.*, 54, n. 124).

In Roman literature miller and baker are interchangeable terms. As wholemeal flour has a shelf life of about six weeks and there is a 60 per cent increase in volume when grain is turned into flour, it makes sense to have milling carried out on the bakers' premises (*ibid.*, 58). It is likely that the military watermills supplied the soldiers just with flour rather than finished loaves, and so may have been plain mills rather than bakeries, but it is not clear if there were any civilian millers who only ground flour for a fee and did not bake bread at all, in the way of millers of the medieval and post-medieval periods. Paying to have grain ground was known in the Roman world; in the novel *Metamorphoses* a donkey-powered mill on a country estate was hired out to grind the grain of neighbouring households, although this was probably done unofficially, as it was arranged by a slave (Apuleius, *Metamorphoses*, 7.15).

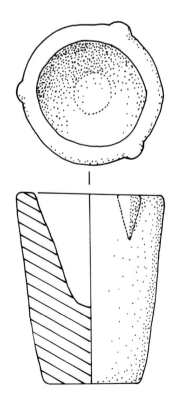

Stone Mortars

Large stone bowls may have been used as mortars to de-husk hulled cereals such as emmer wheat as part of the threshing process (see fig. 12). The bowl stood on the ground and was used with a long wooden pestle.

Fig. 12 Tall stone mortar from Carlisle. (After Padley 1991)

Ethnographic parallels suggest the grain was usually dampened and then pounded by the pestle to separate the grain. The resulting mixture was left in the sun to dry and then winnowed (Nicholson and Shaw 2000, 560). According to Isidore, stone bowls were originally used to grind grain before being superseded by the invention of rotary mills (*Etymologies*, 17.3.45; trans. Barney *et al.* 2006), but they may well have continued in use to process grain which only needed to be crushed rather than finely ground, such as the groats boiled to make coarse porridge. Cato's list of equipment needed for the olive farm includes an iron tube mortar for pounding emmer wheat, a wooden mortar, a fuller's mortar and two unspecified mortars, as well as a pestle for the emmer, a pestle for beans, a pestle for seeds and a pestle to shell nuts, so it is clear mortars could be used for a variety of tasks (*On Farming*, 10).

5

SUPPLY: WOOLWORK

Spinning wool was one activity that was seen to be almost solely women's work. Even rich women, who could escape the actual work, were expected to supervise their slaves at their task, and spinning equipment was often depicted on women's tombstones, or ornamental distaffs of jet or amber were added as grave goods (Cottica 2007; Wild 2002, 8; Wild 1970a, 31–2). Evidence from Pompeii and from literary sources indicates that when cloth production was being carried out commercially men could be involved with preparing the raw wool for spinning and in weaving the finished thread into cloth, but not with the lowlier task of spinning (Moeller 1969; Wild 1967, 659). Graffiti at Pompeii shows that house VII.IV.57 had an area set aside for cloth production which contained three looms, all worked by men, while in the house of M. Terentius Euxdoxus seven male weavers worked beside 11 female spinners (Moeller 1969, 562).

The raw wool first had to be prepared, which seems to have generally been carried out by men. It was usually washed to remove the natural oils in the wool, although they could be left in if waterproof cloth was required for cloaks and capes. If the wool was to be dyed it was done at this stage, still in the fleece (Wild 1967, 659, 661; see *Stockholm Papyrus* 85, 97, 102, 122; *Leiden Papyrus* 98, 99, 101, trans. Caley 1926a and b). It was next combed in order to remove debris from the wool and to straighten the fibres.

The wool was then ready to be spun into thread, using a drop spindle. According to Columella, the farm overseer's wife had to make sure there was a steady supply of wool ready to be spun:

> But in order that she may have recourse to wool-work on rainy days or when, owing to cold or frost, a woman cannot be busy with field-work under the open sky, there should be wool prepared and combed out ready, so that she may be able more easily to carry out the task of spinning and demand this work also from others. (*On Farming*, 12.3.6)

Huge quantities of thread were needed for the loom and spinning would have been a regular task for most women in Roman households. Those that were rich enough could afford to have female slaves spinning thread full time, but in smaller households women would have fitted spinning into their other weekly household tasks. In Egypt, there is evidence that as well as producing thread for their own domestic use, some women made money making thread for professional weavers (Thomas 2001, 14). Other households also had thread spun by outsiders; a second-century letter from Egypt records that about 1.5kg of wool was sent out to be spun (at a cost of 1 *obol* per *stater* [14g]), while the writer spun *c*.2kg of wool herself (Rowlandson 1998, no. 205). Producing enough thread was a lengthy process and the thread would have to be stockpiled until there was enough to start weaving. Where cloth production was carried out commercially it is estimated that at least five spinners would be needed to keep one weaver working full time (Wild 2002, 8).

Slaves would be given a set quantity of wool called 'piecework' (*pensum*) to be spun in a day. Freewomen presumably had more choice over how much they produced during a day, but may still have had a set target to avoid falling behind at a boring task. Whoever was in charge of handing out the piecework could use it as punishment, as suggested by Propertius:'if some talkative slave praises my beauty, she repays her with a greater quantity of piecework' (*Elegies*, 4.7.37; cf. 3.15.15).

The amount spun in a day would depend on the type of thread being produced. A graffito from Pompeii records piecework given to a number of female slaves who were probably working full time at spinning, and mentions thread to be used for the warp (vertical threads on the loom) and for two different types of weft (horizontal threads). The thread would also have to be spun to different thicknesses according to its use, whether for winter or summer clothing, or for wet-weather cloaks or lightweight dining tunics. Fronto, when talking about the spinning activities of the Destinies, says: 'surely no spinner would be so perverse and unskilful as to spin for her master's toga a heavy and knotty yarn, but for a slave's dress a fine and delicate one' (*Correspondence*, trans. Haines 1988, vol. 2, 225). The skill required to produce the different qualities was reflected in their value: in the fourth-century *Edict of Maximum Prices*, 1lb of linen thread of the best quality was worth 1200 *denarii*, while the worst quality of 'coarser linen yarn for the use of common people and slaves' just 72 *denarii* (Graser 1975). Surviving bundles of spun wool from Karanis in Egypt show a range of qualities of workmanship, including one small ball of very fine work (Thomas 2001, figs 18–21).

Piecework was handed out according to weight. In Judaea a wife had to spin five *selas* of warp (71.5g) or ten *selas* of weft (142g) per week for her husband in exchange for the allowance he gave her (*Mishnah*, Nashim, Ketuboth 5.9; pl. 5). Modern parallels suggest this weight of wool would equal approximately 250m in length for a thread that would give 10 to 15 warp threads per inch when woven (info. from Camilla Valley Farm). The quantity woven per day would depend on the type of thread being produced, but it is not clear how much was a typical amount. One modern estimate suggests 110m per hour for wool (Chapman 1972, 20; Munro 2003, 201); some experienced modern hand-spinners can produce about 100m of wool or 36m of linen thread per hour (Carr 2000, 164), while others say approximately 90m per hour (info. from Natural Fibre Company). This would suggest that Jewish women did not spend very long spinning (less than three hours per week if wool, seven hours if linen), which seems unlikely considering how much thread needed to be produced for home-made clothes.

WOOL

The cleaned wool was rolled into a loose roving and wrapped round a stick called a distaff that was 200–300mm in length, often with a circular disc halfway down. Sometimes the wool was loosely tied with thread to keep it in place (see fig. 13). The distaff was tucked under one arm, and the wool was slowly teased out and twisted by attaching it to the spindle, a wooden stick 120–250mm in length weighted at one end, which is then spun round to make it rotate. The weight, or spindlewhorl, is an often bulbous disc made of wood, jet, stone or pottery; in some cultures it was attached to the top of the spindle and in others to the bottom (see figs 13, 14; plate 5). Flat, reused pottery discs pierced by a central hole are common finds on many Roman sites (including military) and are usually identified as spindlewhorls, although the large number recovered suggests they also had other uses, perhaps as some form of tally.

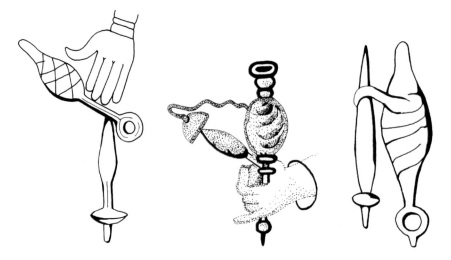

Fig. 13 Spindle and distaffs. Left: from tombstone of Aurelios Trophimos and family, Phrygia, in Römisch-Germanisches Zentralmuseum, Mainz. Middle: Mosaic, La Olmeda Villa, Spain. Right: tombstone, Zagreb Archaeological Museum.

Fig. 15 Wool basket with spun wool. The basket is by the side of the chair of Valerius Celerinus' wife, as shown on his tombstone. (Römisch-Germanisches Museum, Cologne)

Fig. 14 Woman spinning whilst looking after sheep, mosaic from Tabarka, Tunisia.

Thread is teased out until the spindle reaches the floor, when it is then lifted up and the spun thread is wound on to it. The thread is reattached to the top of the stick, and the process starts again. Spinning can be done sitting (see fig. 14; Cottica 2007, figs 36.3–4), standing (when a longer length of thread can be produced before the spindle reached the ground) or whilst walking. Pliny, however, observes that 'a country rule observed on most Italian farms forbids women to twirl their spindles while walking along the road … on the ground that such action blights the hopes of everything, especially the hope of a good harvest' (*Natural Histories*, 28.5.28). When the spindle became full, the thread could be slid off the spindle, the wool could be wound off it into a ball, or it could apparently be left on the spindle, which would require a large number of spindles (see fig. 15).

In the fourth century, the *Edict of Maximum Prices* lists a boxwood spindle, complete with spindlewhorl, as costing 12 *denarii*, and spindles 'of other woods' 15 *denarii*. These were not particularly cheap, at a time when a farm worker earned only 25 *denarii* a day and carpenters, bakers and blacksmiths 50 *denarii*.

Table 4: Average Length of Surviving Distaffs and Spindles

Distaff

Simple wooden	210mm	Wild 1970a, table E
Silver	225mm	British Museum, 1913.0531.6
Jet or amber	260mm	Wild 1970a, table E
Decorated wooden	300mm	Wild 1970a, table E

Spindle

Wood or bone, from north-west provinces	140mm	Wild 1970a, table F
Wood, from Egypt	255mm	Walker and Bierbrier 1997, 330–5

OTHER MATERIALS

Linen was the most common fabric used after wool. The flax was spun in the same way as wool, although a special distaff of reed with a cage at one end was sometimes used (Wild 1970a, 31), and it was spun when damp to create a smooth thread. Other materials include hemp for rope, cotton and the hair of hare, goat, horse and camel, all of which required their own skills for spinning.

BASKET

The wool being worked was kept in a basket, which is often shown sitting by the side of the woman's chair on tombstones, frequently including heavily loaded spindles (see fig. 15; Croom 2000, pls 22–3). Where the distaff and spindle are shown as decorative or symbolic elements outside a figurative scene on tombstones, they are usually accompanied by the basket, which was seen as an equally important part of spinning equipment (Cottica 2007, figs 36.1–2). They are commonly tall, with a wide mouth and narrow base, but a wide variety of designs are shown. A marble imitation of what is assumed to be a cylindrical wool basket was even used as a cremation urn (D'Ambra 2007, fig. 24).

6

MAINTENANCE: CLEANING

Juvenal provides a snapshot of the work involved in preparing a rich man's house in one of his *Satires*:

> When a guest is expected, none of your household will get a break. 'Sweep the marble floor! Polish the columns until they shine! Get that dried-up spider down along with all the web! One of you, wipe the plain silver, and you the embossed vessels'. The master's voice rages as he stands over them, holding the rod. And so you get terribly anxious in case your friend, when he comes, is offended by the sight of your *atrium* fouled with dog turds or the portico splashed with mud, when one little slave boy, equipped with just a half-*modius* of sawdust can put this right. (*Satires*, 14.59)

The tools required to carry out such work are recorded in Roman law, when describing what is included in the *instrumentum* of a house, those items to be sold with a house as being necessary to run it: 'poles with which cobwebs are brushed away, sponges with which columns, pavements and balconies are cleaned, and ladders which are set against panelled ceilings are included among *instrumentum*, because they make the house cleaner' (*Digest*, 33.7.12.22).

The expected arrival of guests or the head of the household after a long absence generally prompted much preparing of the house. In the play *Stichus*, the parasite Gelasimus gets involved in the housework in the hope of a free meal as the slave Pinacium prepares for the arrival of his master (lines 348–55):

> *Pinacium*: Everything must be tidied up. Bring some brooms here, and a long pole, too, so that I can throw out the spider's work entirely, condemn their weaving and discard all their webs.
> *Gelasimus*: Then the poor things will be cold.

Pinacium: What? Think they are like you, do you, with only one outfit? Here, take that broom.

Gelasimus: All right.

Pinacium: I'll sweep here and you sweep there.

Gelasimus: I'm your man.

Pinacium: Will someone bring a watering pot and water?

Gelasimus: He's serving as Superintendent of Public Works without waiting to be elected.

Pinacium: Come you, quick, paint the ground, sprinkle in front of the house.

Gelasimus: I will do it.

Pinacium: It should be done already. Now to knock those spiders off the door and walls!

Gelasimus: By Pollux, business affairs, eh?

Panegyris (wife of the master): I am not at all sure what it all means, unless maybe guests are coming.

Pinacium: Cover the dining-couches, you!

Gelasimus: Dining-couches! Capital start!

Pinacium: Cut firewood, some of you! And you, clean the fish I brought back from my fishing trip. And you – get out ham and sweetbreads!

The level of cleaning in these two quotations could imply that these things were not carried out as a matter of course on a daily basis.

BROOMS AND BRUSHES

According to Pliny 'Castor gave the name "butcher's broom" to the plant *oxymyrsine*, having leaves like a myrtle but prickly, from which they make brooms in the country', while the tamarisk tree was 'of no use except for making brooms' (*Natural Histories*, 23.83.166; 16.45.108). Martial wrote a gift tag for a broom made of palm, but also refers to a slave called an *analecta* who only used their hands (*Epigrams*, 14.82; cf. 7.20.16).

It is not clear whether the brooms mentioned in the literary evidence had long handles in the manner of a modern besom to be used by a person standing up or were simple bundles of twigs that were used by people crouching down, as used in various modern non-western cultures. Cato refers to a broom made of a bundle of dry elm twigs tied to a short handle for cleaning out the massive jars used in winemaking (*On Farming*, 152), so the type was certainly known.

Since one word for 'brush' was simply 'little broom', it suggests some at least were made in a similar way. A number of Roman-period brushes made of palm fibre have survived in the dry conditions of Hawara, Egypt, and while some seem to have been used as large paintbrushes, there are two that might have been used for housework. The simpler example is 19cm long with a circular cross-section, made from coarse fibres folded over and bound with a cord, while the more complex example has a wider, flatter head. It is 27cm long and made of fine palm fibres, bound round once to create the handle, with the head sub-divided into three sections, each tied with fibre cord (see plates 6, 7).

Also surviving from Egypt is a scrubbing brush, made of a rectangular wooden head about 16cm long, drilled with 11 large holes down the long sides and 5 along the short sides apart from the end rows which have 6 holes, through which the bristles are fed (see plate 8). Fragments of a larger example have been found at Vindolanda Roman fort. It consists of an oak frame 23cm long and 19.5cm wide, pierced by a large number of small holes, each one of which holds about 15 to 20 bristles. The bristles are now very short and the brush would have been almost ineffective by the time it was thrown away (see fig.16; Blake 1999, 52). Corner holes in the plate show it was attached to some other element which presumably included a handle of some sort, as it is too large to hold in the hand by itself, unlike the Egyptian example..

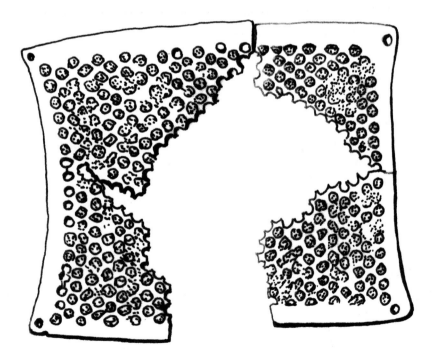

Fig. 16 Wooden and bristle brush from Vindolanda Roman fort.

CLEANING THE FLOOR

Floors in Roman houses ranged from a hard beaten-earth floor to flagstones, bricks, wooden floorboards, mortar or mortar with additional crushed tile (*opus signinum*), shaped marble tiles (*opus sectile*) or mosaics, according to the wealth of the owner and the use of the room. How clean the floor was kept depended on the type of the floor and the status of the room, but in many cases would have been less tidy than would be acceptable now (Davidson 1986, 115–7). Archaeology shows that broken fragments of pottery and animal bones could be included in the material used to make the floors.

It was apparently acceptable to throw unwanted food on to the floor during formal dining, with slaves cleaning tables and sweeping the floor between courses. Martial talks of a miserly man who was not ashamed 'to collect with a long arm what the crumb-collector and the dogs have left'; Horace refers to a slave sweeping up 'the scraps and anything that could offend the guests', while in fiction Trimalchio shows off his wealth by having a dropped silver dish swept away 'among the other rubbish' during his feast (Martial, *Epigrams*, 4. 20.17; Horace, *Satires*, 8.12; Petronius, *Satyricon* 34).

Beaten-earth floors can range from simple compacted mud floors that were dusty when dry and muddy when wet to solid, hard-wearing floors firm enough to stand being washed. In post-medieval Ireland cow dung, lime, ashes or puddled mud scraped from the road were often added to produce a harder surface that raised little dust (Estyn Evans 2000, 60), and in Wales the floors were cleaned with sooty water to create a smooth, shiny surface (Davidson 1986, 119). The addition of ox blood to the mix was also supposed to give it a fine finish. Drawbacks to earthen floors are uneven wear (resulting in patches having to be filled in) and a difficulty in keeping them clean as they absorb any liquid spilt on them.

The other forms of Roman flooring were easier to keep swept or washed. Open fires produced a lot of ash that had to be cleaned away, and Cato recommends that the wife of a farm manager 'must have the hearth ready swept all round each day before she goes to bed' (*On Farming*, 143). General dust and dirt were swept away with brooms made out of thin branches or from palms. Horace mentions other material used in house cleaning: 'Common brooms, cloths and sawdust, how little do they cost! But if neglected, how shocking is the scandal! To think of your sweeping mosaic floors with a muddy palm-broom, or putting unwashed coverlets near Tyrian couch-covers' (*Satires*, 2.4.81–5). The sawdust was used to absorb grease and liquids that could then be swept away; sand has also historically been used for the same purpose and may also have been used in the Roman period. The cloths (*mappa*, meaning napkin or towel) were used to dust or wipe down furniture or household fittings.

Expensive floors such as mosaics, especially those in dining rooms where food and drink were spilt, would also have been washed with water. The *Digest* refers to rooms designed to accommodate this in a section on water rights, observing that a 'hole at the bottom of a wall of a chamber or dining-room, designed for washing the floor, does not imply a right to discharge a steady flow of water' (8.2.28). Evidence from the post-Roman period suggests that the water used for the washing would almost certainly have been cold and used without any form of soap.

CLEANING WALLS AND CEILINGS

The use of open fires and braziers for heating and cooking, and lamps and candles for lighting, resulted in soot collecting on walls and ceilings. One of the explanations Isidore gives for the word *atrium* is that it comes from the word for blackened (*atrum*) 'by fire and a lamp, for the blackening is caused by smoke' (*Etymologies*, 15.3.4, trans. Barney *et al.* 2006). In poorer houses with wattle-and-daub or timber walls and exposed roof beams, little would have been done about the accumulating soot and smoke residues other than perhaps whitewashing the walls periodically. In fiction, authors refer to 'blackened beams' and 'smoky rafters' and 'smoke-stained wall[s]' in the houses of poor country folk (Ovid, *Metamorphoses*, 8, 648; Petronius, *Satyricon*, 135). It was not always considered a bad thing; in later periods it was thought that the smoke from open fires helped to keep the thatch dry and preserve the roof timbers, and that the roofs of buildings without fires soon collapsed (Estyn Evans 2000, 60).

In richer houses with plaster walls, especially painted walls, soot staining was a more visible problem. Vitruvius warned against the dangers when designing buildings:

> In apartments where there is a fire and lamps, the cornices should be plain so that they may be more easily dusted. They can be carved in summer-rooms and open-sided rooms where there is very little smoke, and soot cannot do any damage. For plasterwork, with its glittering whiteness, takes up the smoke that comes from other buildings as well as from the owners.

Fine paintwork and decorative cornices were not recommended in winter dining rooms 'because they are damaged by the smoke from the fire and the frequent soot from the lamps' (*On Architecture*, 7.100.3–4). When Apuleius was accused of performing sacred rites at night in a house rented by a friend called Quintianus, the landlord's evidence was that 'the walls were black with soot', although Apuleius asks how he knew the soot came from these supposed rites, and asks why the slave who had spotted the soot had allowed Quintianus to leave the house without having had it cleaned first (*A Discourse on Magic*, 59). Isidore records that siphons, as well as being used to fight fires, were also used to 'clean ceilings with water forced upwards' (*Etymologies*, 20.6.9, trans. Barney *et al.* 2006).

Soot, consisting of carbon and tar compounds, is made up of very fine particles that can be difficult to remove. It is water repellent, so attempting to wash it away with plain water results in it being smeared even further rather than removed. A detergent needs to be added to the water to wash it away, which in this period probably meant using lye (an alkaline liquid make from wood ash). There is no evidence about how often, if at all, plastered walls were washed, and dingy upper walls and ceilings may have been just a fact of life for the Romans. As walls were usually painted as fresco (whilst the plaster was damp), repainting a room was a major operation, often involving re-plastering the walls, and was only done infrequently.

WASHING WINDOWS

In the early Roman period, windows were glazed with blue-green glass which was translucent, so there was little advantage to cleaning the glass. Windows were often high up the wall, with the result that, if they were washed at all, cloths on long poles or the use of ladders would have been required, both inside and out.

CLEANING FURNITURE AND HOUSEHOLD FITTINGS

On farms, the manager's wife 'must insist the slaves in charge of the *atrium* put out the furniture to air' (Columella, *On Farming*, 12.3.9), but it is not clear how often this was to happen. In the post-medieval period there was often a tradition of an annual 'spring clean', when the house was given a thorough cleaning from top to bottom, but it is not known whether the Romans ever did anything similar. Cato suggests cleaning farm buildings as a task for out-door slaves during wet weather, not as a regular activity but as a way to keep them occupied (*On Farming*, 39.2).

Wood

Cleaning

During and after meals the small round tables had to be cleaned of crumbs and spilt wine. They could be cleaned with cloths (Lucilius, *Satires*, 20.1; Horace, *Satires*, 8.11) or with sponges. Martial wrote a gift tag for one such sponge, describing it as: 'useful for wiping tables when it becomes light and swells after the water is squeezed out' (*Epigrams*, 14.144), and in the play *The Two Menaechmuses* a scrounger is nicknamed Peniculus, meaning a sponge brush, 'because when I eat I sweep the table clean' (act

1, 77–9). Isidore explains the meaning of the word for sponges (*sfungia*) as coming from the word for tidying (*fingere*) 'that is, polishing and cleaning' (*Etymologies*, 12.6.60, trans. Barney *et al.* 2006).

Polishing

Pliny refers to fishes 'with rough skin which can be used for polishing wood and ivory', but their skins were more likely to be used during the manufacturing processes than on an everyday basis (Pliny, *National Histories*, 9.14.40, 32.34.108; cf. the Mishnah, Tohoroth, Kelim 16.2). Roman wooden furniture was not varnished, but could be polished; Cato refers to using the lees of olive oil on it: 'If you rub [it] over all wooden furniture ... it will not decay and polished with this will shine splendidly' (*On Farming*, 98.2). It is possible beeswax was also used, although it is not referred to directly. Pliny gave advice on how to care for the hugely expensive citrus-wood furniture: 'Citrus-wood tables are best kept and polished by rubbing with the dry hand, especially just after a bath; and they are not damaged by spilt wine, as having been created for the purpose of wine tables' (*Natural Histories*, 13.30.99).

Ivory and Bone

As well as rough fish skin, Pliny records that radishes 'can be used for polishing ivory' (*National Histories*, 9.14.40; 19.26.87), and may have also been used to maintain the polish. In Greece, olive oil was used on ivory statues in damp locations (Connor 1998, 54). As bone and antler were used for inlay and fittings in the same way as ivory (and sometimes on the same piece of furniture), it was probably treated similarly as well. Ivory, bone or antler inlaid in furniture would have been polished by the same methods used on the wood.

Metalwork

Rich Roman houses could contain a fair number of metal fittings, such as handles and decorative studs on doors, decorative fittings on couches and boxes, and lamp stands, tables or stools made completely from bronze. The methods of cleaning the metalwork would probably usually be similar to those used for cleaning vessels (see Chapter 6), but also included simple elbow grease: a male slave in the play *Comedy of Asses* by Plautus is told to 'rub these door knobs until they shine' (act 2, 426). Goat-hair cloth, known to have been used by soldiers cleaning their armour, might also have been used to polish bronze in domestic settings (Isidore, *Etymologies*, 18.13.2, trans. Barney *et al.* 2006).

Stonework

A range of coloured stones was used for floor- and wall-coverings in the houses of the rich, either small stones used in mosaics, larger shaped tiles used in *opus sectile* or large sheets of veneer. Stone was also used for household statuary, as well as tables and benches; marble was used where possible, but provincial examples are also known in local materials such as sandstone. The surface was usually polished to bring out the beauty of the stone, fine-grained quartz sand, limestone powder, pumice and emery all being used during the manufacture of stone furniture (Pliny, *Natural Histories*, 36.10.53–4; Isidore, *Etymologies*, 19.13, trans. Barney *et al.* 2006).

Stone floors were probably scrubbed by a brush (see plate 8) using water (modern advice recommends such cleaning just twice a year), then wiped dry and finally buffed with a cloth. Items of furniture may have been cleaned with water and a small quantity of detergent such as lye and then polished with a soft cloth. Stone table tops would have been particularly vulnerable to damage from the mild acids present in wine and in food dishes containing vinegar. Spills would have had to be cleaned as soon as possible as porous stones are easily stained. Such stains could perhaps be removed by pastes including ammonia, with more abrasive cleaners being used only when unavoidable. Modern methods of using pastes usually suggest leaving the paste on for a while to draw stains out (Porter 1987, 27). Statuary that had been painted or had been coated with a hot wax and oil mixture (Vitruvius, *On Architecture*, 7.9.4) would have been treated with care to avoid damaging the finish, and may only have been dusted.

Shale

In Britain shale was sometimes used for three-legged tables and trays as well as platters and containers. Shale is an oil-rich clay, and if the oil is lost the stone starts to laminate and crack, so any items made from it needed to be kept from drying out. The natural colour of the stone is greyish- or brownish-black, but when smoothed and polished with beeswax it can take a very high, black gloss. Items of furniture made from shale would have had to be kept polished, perhaps with wax, to maintain this finish.

COBWEBS

In high-ceiled rooms in the houses of the rich, long poles were used to get rid of cobwebs in not easily accessible places (cf. above; Plautus, *Stichus,* 348–55).

MAKING BEDS AND DINING COUCHES

Roman mattresses were little more than large cloth bags filled with materials such as straw, wool or feathers (Croom 2007, 56–8). This simple design meant that the contents could easily settle down, flatten or grow uneven and lumpy, so they needed to be regularly shaken up as well as aired to keep damp at bay. They would also have to be replaced much more frequently than modern mattresses; in the medieval period the straw in the mattresses of monastic dormitories was changed once a year (Wright 2004, 45). Making a Roman bed or preparing the dining couches would therefore frequently involve plumping up the mattress as well as simply straightening out the bedclothes (Croom 2007, 48, 58). The doctor Soranus recommended nursing women to take exercise that would shake the whole body, but while the rich could play with a ball or throw light weights, 'for those who are poor, however, rowing or drawing up water in a vessel, winnowing or grinding grain, preparing bread, making beds and whatever is done with a certain bending of the body' was suggested (Soranus, *Gynecology*, 2.14 [34], 24[93], trans. Temkin 1956). There is no evidence of how often the bed linens were changed or washed.

GETTING RID OF BUGS AND RODENTS

Flies

Flies would have been a frequent problem in many houses, attracted to open cesspits, rubbish tips and food stored in the open. Sprinkling a room with a decoction of the leaves of the elder plant or with pounded white hellebore and milk was said to kill flies, as would fumigation with the plant Roman coriander (also called blackseed), or smearing coriander seed and olive oil on the walls (Pliny, *Natural Histories*, 24.35.53, 25.25.61, 20.71.184; Scobie 1986, 420). A passage in Lucian's poem *The Fly* explains why olive oil was used: he talks about the creature 'living with man, sharing his food and his table, it tastes everything except his oil, to drink which is death to it' (*The Fly*, 4). It appears that in the Classical world it was thought that insects of all types had a dislike of strong smells or tastes (Panagiotakopulu *et al.* 1995, 706). If these preventatives did not work, then flies had to be kept away by the use of fly whisks and fans (McDonough 1999, 469–70). Martial wrote a gift tag for a whisk made of peacock feathers to keep 'the nasty flies [from] licking your lunch', and also refers to a meal where a slave used a sprig of myrtle as a fly whisk (*Epigrams*, 14.67; 3.82.12).

Fleas and Lice

Environmental evidence recovered during excavations has identified human lice and fleas at Carlisle and York (Kenward *et al.* 1991, 67; Smith and Tetlow 2009, 922; Hall *et al.* 1990, 398, pl. IXa). A probable bedbug has been found in a second-century pit at Alcester, although they appear to have been rare in northern Europe until the post-medieval period (Panagiotakopulu and Buckland 1999, 909–10). The bugs, fleas and lice would have been a potentially major problem mainly in the crowded conditions of the large cities.

In Roman literature they were often equated with the homes of the poor or with crowded public places such as inns. A poor man has a 'bug-trodden bed', a man hiding under a bed in an inn hugged the underside of the bed so tightly he 'pressed his lips even against the bugs in the bedding', while Pliny describes fleas as 'the creatures found in inns in summer time, those that plague us with a quick jump or those that hide chiefly in the hair' (Martial, *Epigrams*, 11.32; Petronius, *Satyricon*, 98; Pliny, *Natural Histories*, 9.71.154). Martial wrote a gift tag for an ivory scratcher for 'when a troublesome flea or anything nastier than a flea' bites (*Epigrams*, 14.83).

Bedbugs are attracted by exhaled carbon dioxide and feed on blood, so in fact the general cleanliness of their surroundings does not actually affect them. However, they spread easily in crowded places, especially if bedding is carried between rooms or partition walls are flimsy, and are difficult to keep under control unless everyone in the building is equally vigilant. During the day they hide in the mattress or pillow, in folds of the bedclothes or further away from the bed in small cracks in the walls, under floorboards, in nearby furniture or behind pictures. They become active at night, especially just before dawn.

There are few successful methods of controlling bedbugs. In the past people have tried washing them away with water, boiling fabrics, soaking furniture in water, fumigating houses with sulphur and pepper, and painting furniture with mercury. Another method was to wait until they appeared at night and then hunt them down by candlelight and crush them one by one, but in the end, if nothing else worked, then the furniture or furnishings simply had to be thrown out (Davidson 1986, 130; Picard 2001a, 117).

The Romans certainly used fumigation to get rid of bugs, and Pliny records a number of recipes. He suggests fumigating rooms with the smoke from leeches roasted in a pottery vessel, or from the smoke of centipedes, while for fleas the smell of burning flowers of freshly gathered pennyroyal was said to be effective (*Natural Histories*, 32.47.136, 29.17.61, 20.44.155). A decoction of the root of the alkanet plant in water or water which had had the young shoots of the elder plant soaking in it could be sprinkled round to kill fleas (*ibid.*, 22.23.49, 24.35.53). He also provided details of how to stop fleas from breeding in the first place, for the more desperate who were willing to try anything: 'if in the spot where the [cuckoo] is heard for the first time, the print of the right foot is marked round and the earth dug out, no fleas breed wherever it is sprinkled' (*ibid.*, 30.25.85). Other recipes for killing bugs were recorded by Varro: 'Soak a wild cucumber in water, and wherever you sprinkle the water the bugs will not come. And again, grease your bed with ox gall, mixed with vinegar' (*On Agriculture*, 1.2.25). A papyrus from Egypt offered other recipes: 'To keep bugs out of the house, mix goat bile with water and sprinkle it. To keep fleas out of the house, wet rosebay with salt water, grind it and spread it' (Parsons 2007, 192).

Moths

Pliny believed it was the dust in wool and clothes that caused moths to breed (especially if there was also a spider in with them, as the spider would drink up all the moisture, making it even drier; *Natural Histories*, 9.41.117). In fact clothing moths prefer damp conditions. They need darkness (as in chests and closets) and are attracted to dirty clothing, especially those containing traces of sweat, urine or spilt drink and food remains. The moth attaches up to 50 eggs to the clothing, which then hatch into the larvae which do the actual damage to the cloth. The larvae spin silken tubes or flat mats in or under which they feed, over a period lasting from a month to two years, before they pupate.

Cato's advice on protecting clothes from moths was to 'boil the lees of olive oil down to half, and with it coat the bottom, the outside, the legs and the edges of the chest. Clothes may be stored in it once it has dried', while Pliny advised storing clothes with wormwood (Cato, *On Farming*, 98.1; Pliny, *Natural Histories*, 27.28.52). In fact, moths are difficult to control and tight-fitting chests that prevented the moths getting in would have been more effective than any form of chemical control.

Rodents

The Romans accepted that mice happily ate food stored by man, and Pliny refers to them as being half domesticated because of their close association with human habitation (Pliny, *Natural Histories*, 8.82.221; Cicero, *On the Nature of the Gods*, 2.63.157–8; Plautus, *The Persian*, 58). As well as eating food, they were a nuisance for their habit of gnawing anything they came across; Pliny records that they were responsible for the death of a general because they had chewed on his puttees (although without explaining how this proved fatal) and he records that mixing an infusion of wormwood in ink would protect anything written with it from hungry mice, while the *Digest* mentions clothes left at the fullers being chewed by mice (*Natural Histories*, 8.82.222, 27.28.52; *Digest*, 19.2.13).

Little is written on how the Romans dealt with mice. Pliny explains that hellebore mixed with pearl barley was said to kill them and the ashes of a cat or weasel dissolved in water (or water in which either of these animals had been boiled) could be sprinkled on agricultural grain stores to drive mice away, but probably most of the time they relied on dogs to kill them, such as those who appear at the end of Horace's tale of the town and country mice (Pliny, *Natural Histories*, 10.94.202, 25.25.61, 18.45.160; Horace, *Satires*, 2.6). While the cat had a traditional role as a mouser in Egypt, and Roman literature refers to mice amongst its prey, it was not as widespread through the ancient world as the dog, and had not yet won its modern reputation as the mouse-catcher *par excellence* (Donalson 1999, 56, 72, 113, fig. 12). Domesticated weasels or polecats might have also been used as mousers in some parts of the empire (*ibid.*, 13, 74). The Mishnah refers to a mousetrap, as does a fable by Phaedrus, but there are no details of what form they took (Tohoroth, Kelim 15.6; Phaedrus, *Fables*, 4.2.17).

7

MAINTENANCE: LIGHTING

The acceptable level of light inside buildings in the ancient world was much lower than that expected in modern western houses, and even during the day, many rooms in Roman houses would have seemed gloomy to twenty-first-century eyes. In poorer houses, windows were often not glazed but simply covered by wooden shutters (in winter requiring a choice between light or warmth), and those that were glazed would often have been small due to the cost of the glass panes. Even in richer households, the use of translucent rather than transparent glass still cut down the amount of light getting through. Doors would often have been left open for the light they let in, but even then many activities now considered to be indoor work would have been done outside. External colonnades allowed work requiring a good level of light to be done outdoors but under shelter, and in early Italian houses looms were set up in the *atrium*, a room with a large roof opening so that there was adequate light for the weaving.

Flaming torches and lanterns were used when outside the house, and lamps and candles inside. The numbers of lamps or candles lit during the evening would depend on the wealth of the family and the activities being carried out. The dining room of a rich family might have multiple lamps hung from a number of lampstands to illuminate the whole room so that the guests could see both each other and the entertainment laid on for them, while a family at home without guests would only need sources of light near where people sat and worked, leaving the rest of the room in darkness. Unlike modern lighting, the sources of light would have needed constant tending when in use, while a frequent household task would have involved refilling lamps with fuel and providing new wicks as necessary, and replacing candle stubs with fresh candles.

OPEN FIRES

In the poorer houses of town and country, and in the barracks of soldiers, the major source of light would often have been no more than the open fire used for cooking and warmth. However, in multi-storey urban apartments and in the houses of the rich, where there were no open fires in a room, other forms of lighting were required.

CANDLES

In the Mediterranean region, where olive oil was cheap, the major source of lighting was the oil lamp, but candles were still widely used. In the first-century novel *Metamorphoses* by Apuleius, for example, a slave raised the alarm when a thief (dressed up as a bear) breaks into a house: 'The darkness was illuminated by torches, lamps, wax candles, tallow candles and every other device for lighting the dark' (4.19), while by the fourth century candles are shown being used to greet the master of the household and to light the way to a bathhouse (see fig. 17; Shelton 1981, pls 3, 6).

Isidore describes a *lucrubum* as a 'small light usually made from a bit of tow and wax', perhaps something like a later rush light, where the wick was covered by just a thin layer of wax. He also refers to cords or papyrus reeds covered in wax or tallow,

Fig. 17 Slaves carrying candles. Left: Silver relief, Esquiline treasure casket. Right: Mosaic, Piazza Armerina villa, Sicily.

which had been used in the past, fixed into holders 'with hooked prongs sticking out' (*Etymologies*, 20.10.8, 20.10.5, 11.2.34, trans. Barney *et al.* 2006).

Manufacture

Candles were made from tallow or beeswax. Making candles was a household task in the countryside, slaves no doubt being pleased to know that the cutting of torches and the dipping of tallow candles were two of the activities that could be carried out on holy days, otherwise meant to be days of rest (Columella, *On Farming*, 2.21.3). A study of candlesticks in Britain has shown that candles were generally quite slim, being only *c.*14–24mm in diameter (Eckardt 2002, 246). These were probably made by dipping. The wick, stiffened by a preliminary coating, was dipped into a pot of molten wax or tallow, withdrawn and allowed to cool and then dipped again and again so that layers built up until the candle was of the requisite thickness. The height of the candle was constrained by the depth of wax or tallow in the vessel, and usually had a distinct taper. A number of wicks attached to a frame meant that multiple candles could be made at the same time, but again, the size of the vessel determined the number.

Thicker candles of beeswax were probably made by pouring, the method used to make large church candles in the medieval and immediate post-medieval period. The stiffened wick was suspended over a container of molten wax and a ladle or similar implement was used to pour the wax quickly down the wick, the surplus wax returning to the container below. While the layer on one wick dried, the wax could be poured over other wicks. This method does not require a deep container and much longer candles could be made. To create a perfect cylinder, the still-warm candle could be carefully rolled on a wet wooden surface. Some late Roman depictions show these much thicker candles (see fig. 17), and a possible Roman wax candle from France had a diameter of *c.*110mm (Bailey 1996, 114, pl. 192).

Images of lit candles tend to show large, unruly flames (see fig. 17), suggesting relatively thick wicks. The wicks for candles and oil lamps could be made from a number of different materials: Pliny lists the inner pith of rushes, papyrus, tow (the outer, inferior layers of flax fibres), a type of phlomis called the 'lamp plant' or the 'wick plant', the interior of oak galls, part of the castor oil plant and a form of sulphur (Pliny, *Natural Histories*, 16.70.178, 21.69.114, 28.47.168, 19.3.17, 25.74.121, 16.10.28, 23.41.83, 35.50.175; Isidore, *Etymologies*, 17.9.73, trans. Barney *et al.* 2006; Dioscorides, *On Medical Matters*, 4.104). The wick made from reeds came from the soft white pith of the common soft rush (sometimes also known as the 'candle rush' for obvious reasons). The reeds were usually collected in summer or early autumn and soaked in water for a while to make the outer case easier to remove. A narrow strip of the case was left in place to keep the pith together. The wicks were left for a couple of days and nights to bleach and absorb some dew, and were then dried, ready for use (Woodward 1935).

Tallow Candles

Most people would have used candles made from tallow (the solid fat extracted from the tissues and fatty deposits of animals) since it was cheap and easily available. The fat was cut up and heated with salted water until it had all melted. The liquid was filtered through a cloth or sieve to get rid of the fragments of cooked meat and gristle and other unwanted debris, and then left to cool; the quality of the tallow depended considerably on how much effort went into this stage. As the mixture cooled, the tallow floated to the surface, where it formed a solid layer which could be removed from the semi-liquid below. The tallow was then ready for use, being heated in the vessel to be used for dipping.

Tallow candles were used until the nineteenth century, and were made from beef, mutton or pig tallow (usually called lard), often mixed together for the best results; mutton tallow was said to give firmness but to be particularly smelly, while pig tallow gave off the most smoke. Traces of animal fat derived from cattle have been found on a Roman candlestick from Cologne (Eckardt 2002, 246).

Tallow candles have a number of drawbacks. They not only have a disagreeable smell, with a flickering, unsteady flame, and produce a lot of smoke, but are also greasy to hold and any drips leave a fatty mark. The wick of a tallow candle only partially burns, so throughout an evening the wick would have to be trimmed to keep the flame bright, using shears or a knife against a hard surface. An experiment carried out in 1789 had shown that the flame of 'an inferior quality' candle after 11 minutes was less than half as bright as when it had been lit (Davidson 1986, 105), although experiments carried out by the re-enactment group *Cohors V Gallorum* in 2008 using good quality tallow did not reproduce these results and the candles were just as bright after half an hour, though the wick did not burn through (see plate 9). Juvenal is probably referring to a tallow candle when he records walking home at night 'by the short-lived light of a candle, whose wick I regulate and tend' (*Satires*, 3. 287).

Wax Candles

Wax candles give a much better light, with less guttering, a more pleasant smell and without the need to continually trim the wick, and were preferred to tallow candles by those who could afford them. The usual method of preparing wax is to heat up broken fragments, cleaned of as much honey as possible, in water so that the liquid wax rises to the surface and any hive debris sinks into the water. When the mixture cools, the wax forms a cake that can be easily lifted away. The wax is then reheated and filtered through cloth to get the finer debris out, as impurities would make the candles splutter and flare (unless the presence of these impurities explains the larger flames shown in art). Pliny records a similar method, using a wicker basket as the filter, and also describes how to make the best white wax: yellow wax is exposed to the wind then boiled with seawater and soda, and the finest white parts scooped off with a spoon. This is boiled with seawater three separate times, then left in the open to be dried by the sun and whitened by the moon before being boiled a final time (*Natural Histories*, 21.49.83–5). This wax was used in particular for medicinal purposes, but the technique was available for the rich who wanted the refinement of white candles. A series of fifth-century funerary mosaics of Christians from Tabarka in Tunisia show that coloured and patterned candles were used for religious or funerary rites (the vertical lines, diagonal spirals and dots were probably painted on the exterior using coloured wax), but it is not known if they were also used in domestic settings.

The large candle being held by the slave ready to greet his master in a mosaic at the villa at Piazza Armenina, Sicily, must be a wax candle (see fig. 17, left), and the more ornate bronze candlesticks which are occasionally found would also have been for wax rather than tallow candles. Wax candles were suitable as Saturnalia presents, and for offering to the gods (a wax candle burning in front of the statue in the Temple of Apollo was responsible for burning the building down: Martial, *Epigrams* 5.18; cf. Statius, *Silvae*, 4.9.40; Aulus Gellius, *Attic Nights*, 4.1.20; Ammianus Marcellinus, *Histories*, 22.13.3). Candles stubs would have been kept so that they could be melted down for reuse (in the eighteenth century, selling wax candle ends was profitable enough to be a recognised as a perquisite of a butler to supplement his wages: Picard 2001b, 120).

Candlesticks

Surviving examples are made out of bronze, iron, lead and pottery, and were made in a wider variety of designs than lamps, although the metal examples most commonly found have three legs (see figs 18, 19). Martial also refers to a wooden candlestick or lampstand (*Epigrams*, 14, 44). Most were freestanding, but iron sockets were sometimes made for sticking into a wall or for suspension by a hook from a beam (Eckardt 2002, fig. 119).

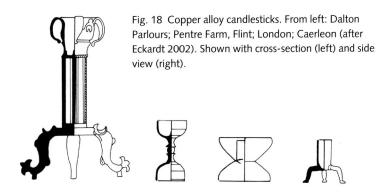

Fig. 18 Copper alloy candlesticks. From left: Dalton Parlours; Pentre Farm, Flint; London; Caerleon (after Eckardt 2002). Shown with cross-section (left) and side view (right).

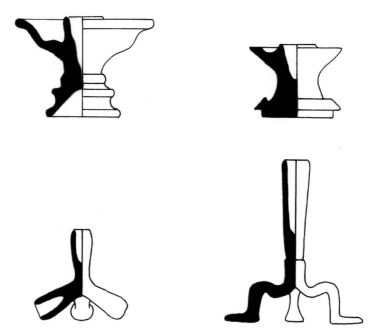

Fig. 19 Candlesticks. Upper row: pottery examples from York (after Monaghan 1997). Lower row: iron examples from Caerleon and Nettleton (after Eckardt 2002). Shown with cross-section (left) and side view (right).

LAMPS

Oil

In those parts of the empire where the olive grew, oil lamps were used extensively, and bronze or pottery lamps are probably the best known of all Roman artefacts. Although they tend to have the same basic design, there was a huge range of decorative detailing and sizes to suit all pockets. Examples with multiple wicks are known, some with up to 14 holes, but the single wick hole was by far and away the most common. For most situations, the light from a single wick seems to have been sufficient, but if more light was required, it was more common for extra one-wick lamps to be lit rather than a multi-wick lamp brought out. Certainly two- and three-wick lamps do not always have correspondingly larger fuel reserves, so the increased burning of the fuel would have required more frequent refilling.

Although olive oil was by far the most common fuel for lamps, in some provinces other forms of oils were used, making use of whatever local resources were available, such as a form of liquid bitumen and the oil from plane-tree berries (Pliny *Natural*

Histories, 35.51.180, 15.7.29; Dioscorides, *On Medical Matters*, 1.99). Residue analysis on lamps suggests hazelnut and walnut oil may also have been used (Eckardt 2002, 36). In those parts of the empire where the olive tree did not grow, the oil had to be imported so stopped being a cheap source of fuel. The level of lamp use varied considerably: in Germany the area round Trier alone has produced over 2700 ceramic lamps, while the whole of Britain has produced only 2600 items of lighting equipment of all types and material, but the exact reasons for such variation is poorly understood (*ibid.*, 28). In Britain oil lamps were used mainly by the military and people living in major urban centres, but the number used, never great in the first place, was already in decline by as early as AD 100 (*ibid.*, 58).

Pottery lamps were not glazed, so they were probably coated with wax or resin to stop the oil permeating the clay and leaving oily marks on whatever surface they rested on. Bronze lamps, although more expensive to buy, had the advantage of being leak-proof. Lamps would have needed a new wick and extra oil either daily or at the very least every few days, depending how much oil they could hold and how long they had been in use. A flame from another source, in the form of a spill, would have been required to light the lamps. The mention of lamps being brought into a dining room part way through a meal might indicate that the lamps were lit in the kitchen or other suitable service room, and were brought to where they were needed ready lit (Apuleius, *Metamorphoses*, 2.19).

In a dinner-party discussion on the reason for not letting lamps be extinguished, Plutarch records an old Roman custom of letting lamps burn themselves out while 'people nowadays put it out directly after eating, so as not to waste oil'. He concludes it was only good manners to leave a lamp burning for anyone else who might need it later. Another guest mentions a man who had the lamps refilled immediately after they had been extinguished, so that he could check they were still full the next day and make sure the oil had not been stolen by the slaves (*Moralia, Table-talk* 7, question 4).

Many of the lamps are quite small and could not hold much oil (the wick of course taking up some additional space). Lamps had 'filling-holes' in the top of their circular body element. In many bronze lamps this hole was quite large and frequently sealed by a small lid (see fig. 20, top row). However, other bronze lamps have the filling hole about the same size as the wick hole, and often much smaller (see fig. 20, lower row). In pottery lamps the filling hole is never larger than the wick hole, and is usually much smaller (see fig. 21), but a noticeable number of lamps have had the hole carefully trimmed back to make it considerably larger, as if their small sizes had annoyed more than a few lamp-users (see fig. 21, lower right). It seems likely that in many instances the oil was poured in through the larger wick hole.

A pottery vessel, with a globular, enclosed body and a low-set, long pouring spout, has sometimes been identified as a possible lamp filler for pouring the oil into the lamp, but the form has also been identified as a feeding bottle for children or invalids

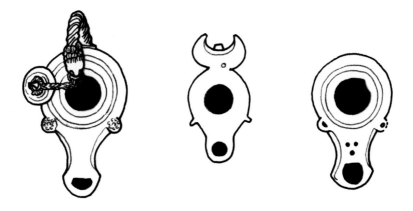

Fig. 20 Bronze oil lamps, showing a range of styles of filling holes.

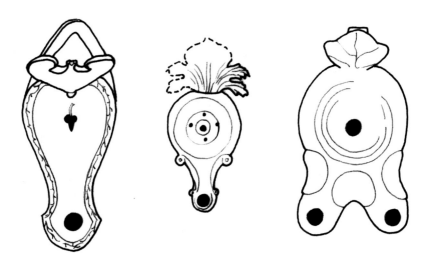

(Eckardt 1999, 70–1). In fact, any small pottery or glass vessel can be used with care as a lamp filler, especially as the slightly concave top surface edged with a slight ridge found on many lamps helped spilt oil drain through the hole(s) as long as no one minded a slightly sticky lamp (see plate 10).

Oil lamps provide a steady, clear flame, although too-long wicks produce smoke, and the burning fuel smells. When Juvenal describes the drawbacks of being a schoolteacher he advises: 'just make sure you get something for breathing the stink of as many lamps as there are boys, while your Horace gets totally discoloured and the soot sticks to your blackened Virgil' (*Satires*, 7, 225–7). Perfumed oil was occasionally burnt in lamps, but it does not seem to have been a common practice (cf. Martial, *Epigrams*, 10.38.8; Petronius, *Satyricon*, 70).

The wick does not need to be tended as often as that of a tallow candle, but every few hours or so it would have needed to have been pulled up. This can be tricky, to avoid putting out the flame, and a long pin or similar is needed (which also comes in handy for feeding a new wick in through the wick hole). A farmer lighting a lamp from the embers of a fire 'draws out with a pin the dried-up wick, and with many a puff wakes up the sluggish fire' (Anonymous, *Moretum*, 10–2). Since almost anyone using a lamp would need some way of pulling up lit wicks, some of the many objects identified as hair or dress pins in the archaeological record may have originally been intended for this purpose, although there is no way of recognising them. The first-century engineer Hero of Alexandria, who invented various mechanical devices, designed a lamp with an automatic wick feeder (Humphrey *et al.* 1998, fig. 10), but it was not adopted for daily use, and the design of lamps in fact changed little throughout the Roman period.

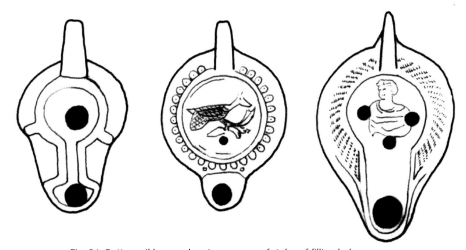

Fig. 21 Pottery oil lamps, showing a range of styles of filling holes.

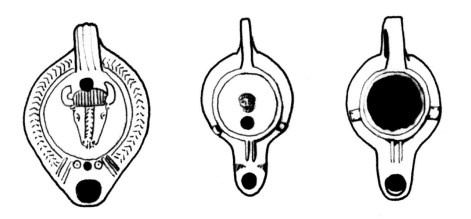

An experiment carried out by the re-enactment group *Cohors V Gallorum* using a small replica lamp which could hold *c.*65ml of oil (just over four tablespoons) showed that with good quality olive oil and a flax wick it would burn about 17ml of oil in an hour and use 1-2cm of wick (plate 10). Even a small lamp, therefore, could burn for between three and four hours, or much of an evening, before needing to be refilled. Larger lamps would only have to be refilled on a daily basis, and new wicks supplied even less frequently.

Fat

Open lamps made of pottery, iron, lead or even stone were also used. Iron lamps, hanging from a long hooked rod that could be driven into a wall, were common in Britain. The lamps are attached loosely to the bar so that the bar could be hung (or carried) vertically or horizontally, as seen in illustrations of the (closed) lamps used by the men who dug the catacombs (see figs 22a, 22b). Such open lamps are often called 'crusies', after the later Scottish lamps usually fuelled by fish oil, and it is assumed they were used with animal fats such as tallow (the rendered fat of beef or sheep), lard (from pigs) or dripping (the fat melted from cooking meat). However, the lamps can only be used with liquid fats; solid fats cannot flow towards the flame or be drawn up the wick, so the flame either goes out when the available fuel has been used up or the full length of the exposed wick lying on the bottom of the lamp starts to burn (see plate 11).

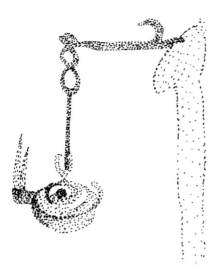

Fig. 22a Hanging oil lamp in use. From a wall painting showing a catacomb digger at work, Catacombs of S. Marcellinus and Peter, Rome.

Fig. 22b Iron hanging open lamp, Newstead Roman Fort.

Experiments showed that if hot fat is poured into an iron lamp it heats the lamp enough to keep the fat liquid for several hours, but poured into a pottery lamp it only warms the pottery marginally and the fat soon solidifies.

PREVENTING FIRES

Lighting by candles and lamps has always been dangerous. In the nineteenth century 65 per cent of fires in London with known causes were started by candles (Davidson 1986, 102) and even today the fire brigade warns against the dangers of leaving burning candles untended. Add in open fires, portable braziers and under-floor heating, and there were many opportunities for fires to start in Roman houses. One of the duties of the Prefect of the City Guard of Rome was, according to the law, to give a severe dressing-down and warning to those who 'kept their fire too carelessly' or even to have them beaten with sticks or flogged, 'as very often houses go on fire through the negligence of the occupiers' (*Digest*, 1.15.3–4).

While some large cities had companies of firemen, they were not organisations with the same remit as modern fire services and the majority of people in the empire had to rely on their own efforts, and hopefully those of their friends and neighbours, to put out any house fire. When Pliny reported on an extensive fire in the city of Nicomedia he recorded that there were no firemen, no public siphon and no water buckets or other apparatus for fighting fires, and that the fire spread as far as it had because people just stood around watching it without trying to do anything (*Letters*, 10, 33, 2). He asked for permission to set up a company of firemen, but the Emperor was afraid such a group of men would turn into a political club and said that 'it was a better policy to provide the equipment necessary for dealing with fires, and to instruct property owners to make use of it, calling on the help of the crowds which collect', slightly optimistically perhaps, considering the town folk had already proved themselves unwilling to get involved (*ibid.*, 10, 34).

Individual house owners or occupiers were supposed to keep their own fire-fighting equipment to hand. The Prefect of the City Guard of Rome 'was under orders to warn everyone to have a supply of water ready in an upstairs room' in case fire broke out (*Digest*, 1.15.3), while the law included objects intended for fighting fires as part of the *instrumentum* of a house (those items required to make a house run properly and therefore not to be sold separately). Thus the *instrumentum* included 'vinegar, which is intended to put out fires … likewise rags, siphons, also poles and ladders, sponges, water-buckets and brushes' (*ibid.*, 33.7.12.16–8).

8

MAINTENANCE:
DOING THE WASHING UP

At the end of every meal there were the cooking and table vessels to be cleaned. This was another activity that was just as likely to be carried out by men as by women. Juvenal talks of male slaves 'washing the dishes and puffing at the embers with full cheeks, clattering the oily strigils, filling the oil flasks and arranging the towels', unaware that their master has just died in a road accident (*Satires*, 3. 261–3). The modern interpretation of 'washing up' involves the use of water in the process, but not all the methods used in the past required it. Based on later practices, much of the time vessels (and no doubt cutlery) would have just been wiped over with bread or straw before being put away, while communal cooking pots may rarely have been emptied to be cleaned (Davidson 1986, 133). Washing up was not a topic that usually interested Roman authors, but luckily some of the works on farming refer to the methods used to clean farm equipment, and it is assumed that similar methods could also have been used in domestic surroundings.

The vessels to be cleaned can be divided between those that had been used to cook the food and those used to serve it. For many people in the Roman period food was cooked in unglazed pottery vessels over an open fire, so the outer surfaces were covered in soot whilst the inner surfaces absorbed fats, and those used for boiling water got a coating of limescale in hard-water areas. Larger cooking vessels were made out of bronze, but only occasionally iron, which seems to have been restricted on the whole to small frying pans and oversized cauldrons.

Tableware was available in a wider range of materials, starting with wooden vessels for the poor, and then, in approximate order of expense, the same coarse-ware pottery that was used for cooking, vessels made from finer clays not intended for use over a fire (called 'fine wares'), glass, copper alloy, pewter and silver. As nowadays, the cleaning methods were divided between those suitable for getting rid of grease and easily removed crumbs or liquids, typically using water with or without an added detergent, and those needed to remove burnt-on food or heavy sooting by the use of an abrasive.

Cooking over wood or charcoal resulted in vessels dirty on the outside from the soot and smoke. When the poet Venantius Fortunatus talks venomously about a cook who had wronged him, he describes him as 'black-hearted, smoke-fed, soot-dyed: his face is another cooking pot which his own implements have painted a filthy colour – frying pans, pots, bowls, plates, trivets; unworthy of being marked by verse rather than by soot, may his foul image reflect the pitch-black man' (*Poems*, 6.8, trans. George 1995). Sherds of cooking pots found on archaeological sites can have heavy soot deposits on their exteriors, suggesting the exterior may not always have been fully cleaned.

Some of the vessels to be cleaned would have required careful attention. Delicate glass or decorated silverware was not suitable for scouring with an abrasive, while others had protective coatings that needed to be treated with care. Wooden vessels were often coated with a layer of wax, and coarse pottery vessels could have an inner layer of wax, clay slip, gum or resin to stop liquids seeping into the clay, which had to be protected during any washing process. Pitch was used for vessels containing wine, a seawater mixture called *thalassomeli* and Egyptian soda (Columella, *On Farming*, 12.29; Pliny, *Natural Histories*, 31.35.68, 31.46.114). Containers for olive oil and preserved olives were more often treated with gum, wax or the lees from olive oil production (Columella, *On Farming*, 12.49.11, 12.52.16–7; Cato, *On Farming*, 100). In Judaea vessels for 'fish-brine' were 'lined with gypsum up to the brim' (Mishnah, Tohoroth, Kelim 10.5). These vessels were used for storage, but smaller containers in the house would also have been treated in the same way. Persius mentions a decanter of wine spoilt because the pitch had gone bad and Horace commented that jars will keep the fragrance of whatever had been put in them when new (Persius, *Satires*, 5.146–7; Horace, *Epistles*, 1.11.69–70).

METHODS

Pure Water

Cold water was sometimes used for cleaning even greasy items, although this demanded patience. If hot water was not required, then the washing, like clothes washing, could be carried out outside near a water source so that there were large quantities of constantly replenished clean water. Columella describes how to clean the frails (wicker containers) used in oil presses; after they had been used they should be:

washed out immediately two or three times in very hot water; then, if there is running water at hand, they should be sunk in it having heavy stones put on top of them … or if there is no stream, they should be soaked in a lake or pond of the purest possible water and afterwards beaten with rods that the dirt and lees may fall off them. (*On Farming*, 12.52.22)

He also records that large jars being prepared for the new wine crop had to be 'scoured and carefully washed with sea-water or salted water and properly dried'; the seawater was preferred to the fresh water (*ibid.*, 11.11.70, 12.18.3).

Lye

It was easier to clean greasy items in water with added detergent. A detergent can be made by adding an alkali to the water, as alkalis make grease or oil more soluble in water and therefore easier to clean. Lye was one such detergent, being water containing alkaline salts extracted from wood ash. Lye was made by running water very slowly through layers of wood ash. There were various ways of doing this, but a nineteenth-century description gives the basic idea: a layer of clean straw was placed on the bottom of a wooden frame, covered by a large coarse cloth, which was in turn covered with a thick layer of wood ash. The frame was then filled with water, which over the course of a few days slowly filtered through to a container placed below (Davidson 1986, 142). The resulting liquid was the lye, ready for use. A Roman description of making lye comes from a recipe for preserving grapes, and refers to 'cinders of brushwood ash in a bronze vessel or a large new earthernware pot' (Columella, *On Farming*, 12.16.1). Columella, in describing how to clean out jars used in the production of olive oil, said that they should be:

cleaned out and washed out once and again with lye, which should not be very hot, lest they should lose their wax [coating], and then they should be roughly rubbed with the hands in tepid water and rinsed out several times and all the moisture dried out with a sponge. (*On Farming*, 12.52.14–7)

Sand

In the post-Roman period sand, or other finely ground stone such as granite powder, was used to remove food sticking to the pan such as burnt-on remains or the residue of thick stews or sauces. Scouring the vessels with sand also had the advantage of polishing the vessel at the same time as cleaning it. The sand would have had to be sourced and then transported to the home and stored until required. City dwellers, lacking easy access to sources of sand, either had to buy it, as happened in the seventeenth and eighteenth centuries, or else use an alternative such as wood ash (Davidson 1986, 122, 125). The sand or other stone was rubbed into the vessel using a bit of cloth. When the vessel was clean, the last few grains of sand could be brushed off by hand or rinsed off with water, although this job was sometimes left to just before the vessel was next used.

Other Materials

Large jars being cleaned for reuse were scraped with 'brushes of dry elm twigs bound around a stick' (Cato, *On Farming*, 152), and small brushes of twigs, leaves or palm fibres might have been used in a domestic setting. In the post-Roman period other methods of cleaning vessels included the use of twists of straw and of bran (the bran absorbed the food remains and could then be fed to the pigs: Davidson 1986, 125) and it is likely there were similar local methods used throughout the Roman Empire.

RE-LINING AND REPLACING POTS

Although many vessels were lined by professionals before they were sold (a papyrus even records a pottery worker warning his employer that other workers were wasting money by giving the pots two coatings of pitch: Cockle 1981, 90, 94), the job would also have been done on the farm as the vessels would require periodic re-lining, with the large wine storage vessels needing to be done every year (Peña 2007, 211). Columella said that pots used in producing olive oil used to be re-waxed after every sixth harvest, but added: 'I do not understand how this can be done, for while new vessels, if they are heated, readily admit the wax, yet I cannot believe that old vessels, being saturated with oil-juice, can bear the application of wax' (*On Farming*, 12.52.15–7).

Horace mentioned that unless a vessel was clean then whatever was poured into it would turn sour (*Epistles*, 1.11.54), and pottery vessels would often have been replaced not because they had been broken but because they had turned rancid. Brand-new vessels were often specified when preserving or preparing food, including olives in oil, raisins, pomegranates, ground barley, goose fat and starch (Columella, *On Farming*, 12.50.1, 12.16.1, 12.46.6; Pliny, *Natural Histories*, 18.14.74, 29.39.134; Cato, *On Farming*, 87). Modern glazed pottery can have a very long life, but in the past unglazed pottery was seen as much more disposable. Eventually there was no point in trying to clean a pot any more, and it was better to throw it away and use a new one in its place.

LOCATION

The one possible depiction of a Roman doing the washing up comes from a tombstone called the Igel Monument in Germany, in a scene showing male slaves at

Fig. 23 Male slaves at work in a kitchen. Stone relief on the Igel Monument, Germany.

work in a kitchen (see fig. 23, plates 12,13). To the right, one man holds a large pan over the raised hearth while a second slave pours a tub of something (food or water?) into it. Next there is another slave bent over a large round bowl set on a small square table covered with a cloth. He is either grinding up food in a mortar or cleaning residue from a cooking pan; whatever he is doing, his arm lying round its rim to anchor it and his bent back show he is put some effort into it. Next there is a slave at a large rectangular table which has two large serving dishes set out on it. He has a knife in hand and is cutting up some form of food, but is looking over his shoulder at the final slave, who is drying or polishing a serving dish with a large cloth. A second scene on the same monument that has a central scene of the family dining shows slaves serving drinks from a side table to the left while to the right a slave carries a dish away from the table and a second wipes or polishes one of two large serving dishes on a work table (see plate 14).

While the washing up could be carried out in a kitchen (or where the food was prepared and cooked in dwellings without separate kitchens), Roman kitchens did not have sinks so washing up was not confined to any one room, and could easily be done outside. This had the advantage that water was not splashed about inside and the waste water could be poured straight on to the ground and dirtied sand thrown aside. When washing up was done inside the water had to be collected, either straight from an outside source or from water jars filled earlier in the day or, in well-appointed kitchens in large establishments, from built-in water storage tanks (see fig. 10). Usually the washing up was carried out on a table, in a container of a suitable size (due to a lack of pottery ones of an appropriate design in the archaeological record such containers were probably of wood). Scouring vessels would require sand or other abrasive material being sourced and brought inside in a container, such as a bucket or sack, and stored until needed.

POLISHING METALS

As well as cleaning away food residues or soot, scouring would also help to polish metal vessels. To polish the metal to a high shine, finer-grained material would be used, such as fine earths or ashes. In the play *The Braggart Soldier* by Plautus, a woman's words are described as 'needing no ashes' because they are already 'elegant and polished' (999–1003).

Copper and Bronze

Roman bronze was made from copper with approximately 10 per cent tin and a small quantity of lead, the exact proportion of which depended on what the metal was to be used for (Strong and Brown 1976, 26, 39). Alloys without lead were used for vessels raised from sheet metal, but up to 30 per cent lead was included for the cast elements of vessels such as handles (*ibid.*, 40). Brass was made of copper with added zinc rather than tin, and had a more golden colour. Bronze implements can be divided between those used in the kitchen, at the table and for bathing. Those for use in the kitchen included pots for boiling water or cooking food over a fire, moulds used in ovens and implements such as food graters for preparing food (Allison 2004, fig. 5.11). Vessels designed for the table included jugs for liquids, and dishes, pans and plates for serving food (*ibid.*, figs 4.17, 8.5). Bronzes designed for washing were decorated buckets and large bowls for holding water, small scoops for pouring water, and jug and shallow bowl sets used for hand-washing (*ibid.*, figs 4.15–6). Cleaning requirements therefore ranged from removing soot and baked-on food to washing away the traces of acidic wine and food dishes that had contained such ingredients as oil, vinegar or honey, which could affect the metal if left in contact with it.

One of the duties of the overseer's wife on a farm was to make sure that 'bronze utensils are scoured and polished and freed from copper-rust' by the slaves (Columella, *On Farming*, 12.3.9). Copper rust, or *verdigris*, is a green coating that develops when copper is exposed to the air, especially when it is humid or there are sulphides present (creating a form of copper carbonate), or when acid reacts with the copper surface (creating a more harmful copper acetate). If a vessel is used for food or drink when the metal is covered with *verdigris* there is the danger that the food will dissolve this coating, which at the very least spoils the flavour (cf. Columella, *On Farming*, 12.20.1–2) and at worse leads to mild food poisoning and upset stomachs. However, as the Romans continued to serve acidic wine in narrow-necked jugs whose inner surfaces could never have been cleaned easily, there must have been some way round this danger. Cooking vessels were sometimes lined with tin or a tin alloy to give 'the contents a more agreeable taste and to prevent the formation of destructive verdigris'; modern copper pans are usually coated with tin (Pliny, *Natural Histories*, 34.48.160; Beagrie 1989, 170).

To clean objects made of copper alloy, materials such as ashes, alum or finely crushed pumice may have been used, being less abrasive than sand and therefore preserving a high shine (Pliny, *Natural Histories*, 33.20.65). The regulations for the bathhouse at an imperial mining facility in Spain dictate that every month the manager should 'properly wash, scrub, and polish with fresh fat the bronzes that he uses' (Fagan 2002, no. 282). Cato recommended coating bronze items with the lees of olive oil after they had been cleaned thoroughly to preserve the polish: 'Apply the *amurca*, and clean them when they are to be used. They will be shinier, and they will be protected from verdigris' (*On Farming*, 98.2). Others recommended leaving the metal coated at all times. Pliny records that 'things made of copper or bronze get covered with copper-rust more quickly when they are rubbed clean than when they are neglected, unless they are well greased with oil. It is said that the best way of preserving them is to give them a coating of liquid vegetable pitch' (*National Histories*, 34.21.99). The third-century *Leiden Papyrus*, a series of chemical recipes, includes one for 'cleaning copper objects': 'Having boiled some beets, carefully clean the objects of copper and silver with the juice. The beets are boiled in water' (recipe 46, trans. Caley 1926a).

Silver

Any Roman family with pretensions to wealth would have had silver plate in their house. In the Roman period, silverware was divided between silver for drinking out of (jugs, cups, ladles and wine-mixing bowls), eating off (plates, bowls and spoons), for show (bowls and similar intended for display only) and for toilet (mirrors, buckets, bowls, jugs and scoops, for use both in the bathhouse and for washing hands and feet at the table). Sets used in the dining room helped to demonstrate the host's social status, and extra pieces were frequently laid out on side tables for the guests to admire, often including dishes with decorative three-dimensional figures located on the inside which could only have been used for display. A set of silver plate found in the House of Menander in Pompeii, thought not to be the 'best' set used for formal dining, still contained 118 pieces weighing 23.5kg of silver which would have cost 35,000 *sesterces* for the metal alone (Painter 2001, 26, 41).

Some silver vessels, particularly drinking cups and display dishes, could be highly decorated with strongly modelled relief. The cups usually had a very thin outer skin that could be worked in deep relief, and a thicker inner lining that gave the cup more strength and provided a smooth interior surface. Such thin three-dimensional moulding would require great care to clean properly without damaging the artwork or leaving residues from the cleaning materials. It was likely that only certain trusted slaves were allowed to clean the silverware; in large households there would be a slave whose sole job was to look after it.

Silver is affected by many ingredients commonly found in food, including sulphur-containing food such as eggs, salt and acids such as vinegar and fruits. To avoid tarnishing, silver should be cleaned immediately after use, when water and detergent are usually enough to keep it clean. Unused or uncleaned silver gradually grows dull and turns black as it reacts with sulphur in the environment, and requires stronger cleaning methods. Since silver can be easily scratched, modern techniques recommend non-abrasive methods of polishing, with even a traditional recipe such as water and bicarbonate of soda paste sometimes considered too harsh. The Romans, however, were apparently not so concerned; silver was polished with white marl or another fine white earth called silversmith's earth (*creta argentaria*; Pliny, *Natural Histories*, 17.4.45, 35.26.44, 35.57.199). The black surface on silver could also be 'rubbed off with vinegar and chalk' (*ibid.*, 33.46.131). The *Leiden Papyrus* includes the instruction 'to clean [it] with sheep's wool, after having dipped in sharp brine, then clean with sweet water and put into use', and also suggests using moist alum and beet water (recipes 48, 66, 46, trans. Caley 1926a).

Pewter and Tin

Roman pewter vessels were made from tin alloys that ranged in composition from almost 100 per cent tin to alloys with less than 40 per cent tin (Beagrie 1989, 172, fig. 1). When new, pewter is the colour of silver, but oxidises to a dull grey, which in some periods was the preferred finish. However, as high-lead alloys seem to have been used as cheaper alternatives to silver or silver-alloy vessels in the Roman period, it is likely they were intended to be kept polished (*ibid.*, 173). Pliny mentions mirrors made of tin alloy, as well as a variant called 'silver mixture' used for plating any type of object, and a Gallic method for plating bronze items 'so as to make them almost indistinguishable from silver' (*Natural Histories*, 34. 47.160–3). As pewter can be stained and pitted by acidic food, it would have to be cleaned soon after use, and as it is easily bent and scratched, it would have to be cleaned with care. No Roman method for cleaning pewter survives, but the *Leiden Papyrus* includes a recipe for cleaning tin that would have also been suitable for pewter: 'place some gypsum on a rag and scour' (recipe 65, trans. Caley 1926a).

Iron

Knives were the most common form of domestic utensils made of iron, but large ladles, frying pans and occasionally cauldrons were also known. Stainless steel was unknown in the Roman period so most iron implements took on a dull grey colour unless specifically and repeatedly polished to a silver finish. Iron knives, unless dried immediately on washing, end up with orange rust marks which can be quite easily wiped away. Left too long, however, and the metal will start to rust in earnest, leaving a pitted surface. Rust, according to Pliny, could be cleaned by using seawater (*Natural Histories*, 31.33.66). Alternately, iron items could be given a protective covering such as lead acetate, gypsum or vegetable pitch (*ibid.*, 34.43.150). Isidore adds that 'rust does not damage iron implements if they are smeared with deer marrow or white lead mixed with oil of roses'(*Etymologies*, 16.21.7, trans. Barney *et al.* 2006). Knife blades would also have been periodically sharpened with the use of a whetstone, and Pliny lists the sources of a number of whetstones, commenting on their reputation and whether they should be used with oil, water or a mixture of both for maximum efficiency (or just saliva, as used by barbers, who had a reputation for using blunt blades; *Natural Histories*, 36.47.164–5).

CLEANING WOOD

Wooden vessels would have been used more extensively in areas where there was less of a native tradition of pot-making. Roman writers from the Mediterranean region usually equated wooden utensils either with the poor or with a more austere, less materialistic past (Martial, *Epigrams*, 12.32.13; Valerius Maximus, *Memorable Sayings*, 4.3.5), but the archaeological record shows that richer people also sometimes bought wooden utensils of superior workmanship or made from exotic woods. The Romans favoured strongly patterned woods, so burrs were particularly fashionable and were used for two vessels found in Britain. Boxwood burr was used for a fine bowl found at the Fishbourne palace and elm or walnut burr was probably used for a handled cup from Cramond Roman fort. A number of very thin-walled platters of very high-quality craftsmanship from Herculaneum were also clearly not utilitarian kitchen ware (see fig. 24; Pugsley 2003, 103, 108).

Flasks, cups, bowls, platters, mortaria, bread-making troughs, ladles, scoops and spatulas were all made from wood. Pieces have been found made from a wide range of woods, including alder, ash, beech, boxwood, conifer, dogwood, elm, fruit trees (such as apple or hawthorn), hazel, larch, lime, maple, oak, willow and yew (*ibid.*, 103, 113, 117, 137, 175; Martial, *Epigrams*, 12.32). The yew was used for a lid or bowl; Pliny refers to a yew-wood water flask poisoning drinkers, although the poison in yews is mainly concentrated in the leaves, seeds or bark and not the wood (*Natural Histories*, 26.20.50).

Many wooden utensils would simply have been wiped clean rather than washed, but if necessary they could have been washed with water and detergent. They cannot be soaked in water or have liquids left in them for any length of time as there is the risk of them warping or splitting. They need to be oiled every once in a while to stop them from drying out, and the Romans seem to have used the lees of olive oil for

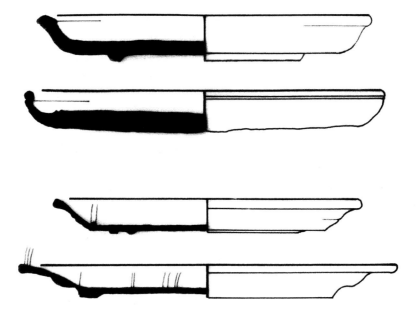

Fig. 24 Wooden dishes. From top: from the *Fortuna Maris* wreck, Italy; Carlisle; and two from Herculaneum. (After Pugsley 2003)

this where it was available (Pliny, *Natural Histories*, 15.8.34). In modern times, olive oil or lard has sometimes been used, but wood turners point out that both can turn rancid, and if too much builds up over time the vessels turn sticky and unpleasant to use. The residue can be removed by the use of an abrasive and some detergent, and the seasoning started again. Beeswax was also used in the Roman period; Ovid mentions a peasant couple bringing out 'cups of beech-wood coated on the inside with yellow wax' for their guests (*Metamorphoses*, 8, 670).

9

MAINTENANCE: CLEANING CLOTHES

INTRODUCTION

B efore the invention of washing machines and tumble dryers, washing clothes was a very labour-intensive activity and could take a considerable time to complete. The poor, with few changes of clothes or household linens, usually had to wash their garments weekly, but richer establishments which possessed multiple changes of linen (and in country houses the space to dry it) could let the dirty laundry collect for longer and carry out a monthly or six-weekly wash instead (Davidson 1986, 150; Picard 2001a, 115). In the 1840s washing and ironing for a family of 10, carried out on a monthly basis, took four full days; even in poorer families, where the wash was carried out weekly, it could still take two days (Davidson 1986, 152). One day of the week was usually set aside for washing, involving an early start (1 a.m. or 3 a.m. were not unknown, every week year in, year out) and usually also the neglect of other household tasks, such as cooking hot meals, in order to get the washing done and out of the way. The poor had to do their washing by themselves, but anyone who could afford it preferred to hire a washerwoman, either to come to their house or to take the washing away to do in her own house. The rich could afford to have full-time washerwomen or could send out their washing to professional laundry establishments.

Wash days were often viewed with dread, since the work was hard and unpleasant but unavoidable. They involved very long hours of heavy work, constant splashing and dampness, working with cold water even in midwinter, carrying the heavy weight of the wet cloth and the smell of the cleaning agents. The clothes needed to be laid out to dry, requiring a constant attention for the dangers of passing rain showers, or else finding alternative ways of drying them on wet or freezing days, especially during the winter. Even after drying, the work was not finished, as the clothes and linens then needed to be pressed, folded and put away.

Until very recently, washing was divided between those items that needed to be washed frequently (usually items that came in contact most with the skin, such as underclothes, sheets and towels) and those that only occasionally needed cleaning or simply spot removal (ibid., 1986, 137). The first category consisted of items that were frequently made of either linen or cotton that was usually bleached rather than dyed, and the second category fabrics such as wool, velvet, brocade and other elaborate materials that were usually dyed.

FREQUENCY

It is not clear how often the Romans washed their clothes. Washing the human body was a major leisure pursuit at the time, while it was considered important in Mediterranean society to look 'well-washed' (Bradley 2002, 23), so the rich may well have demanded a steady supply of clean clothes. However, the damaging nature of the cleaning methods employed at the time may have meant that the same clothes were perhaps worn for several weeks before being cleaned, rather than days (Bradley 2002, 29, n. 76). In the early fifth century, Augustine warned a community of nuns against the excessive desire for clean clothes: 'let your clothes be washed, either by yourselves or by the fullers, at the discretion of the superior, so that excessive solicitude for clean clothes may not infect the soul' (Letters, 211; the nuns themselves were only allowed to use the baths once a month: ibid., 209). As washing took its toll on the clothes by both damaging the cloth and fading any dye, the poor may not have washed their clothes too often.

Clothes were expensive in the Roman period, to the extent that they were worth stealing and were often included in wills, so the number of times clothes were washed helped identify their worth; in the novel Satyricon the slave house steward pretends he is not too concerned about a set of clothes stolen from the bathhouse because 'they have been washed once already' (Petronius, 30), and Martial mentions a gift of a toga 'washed three or four times at the most' (Epigrams, 10.11). There is some evidence that pale-coloured clothes were cleaned more often than darker clothes as any stains were more obvious (Bradley 2002, 29), so the outer appearance was sometimes more important than genuine cleanliness.

THE CONTENTS OF THE LAUNDRY

The most frequently washed items would have been made of undyed linen that could take the rough methods of washing, and, least frequently, thick woollen items such as blankets, heavily decorated bedcovers or dining-couch covers, and thick bad-weather cloaks and capes. Under-tunics, probably usually made from linen, would have been washed more often than outer tunics, and expensive clothing such as togas and decorated woollen tunics would have been cleaned only when necessary. Silk clothes and delicate cloths so fine they were semi-transparent would have required different methods and great care to avoid damaging them.

The most frequent washing would have been required for bed linens, towels, napkins and the clothes worn closest to the skin. As well as under-tunics, these would have included loincloths for men, bra-bands for women and socks for both sexes. In addition, swaddling clothes, menstrual cloths and handkerchiefs would have needed more regular washing than clothing.

Nappies and Similar

Babies were kept wrapped in swaddling clothes from their birth until they were 40 to 60 days old, the exact date depending on when the body seemed to have become 'firm' enough (Soranus, *Gynecology* 4. 42[111], trans. Temkin 1956). Swaddling clothes were designed to control and mould the body to a 'correct' shape, and could take a number of different forms. Soranus describes one arrangement made up of two pieces of cloth, one large enough to cover the whole body and the other 'large enough for the reception of the faeces to go round the loins only' (*ibid.*, 2.14[83]). It is not clear how often either the swaddling or 'nappy' were changed; in later periods nappies could be kept on for a couple of days, and swaddling for weeks. Nor is it known if nappies were used by themselves after the swaddling was no longer needed. In warm countries it was, and still is, common to leave the child naked, with the mother learning to anticipate its bowel movements and hold it over a suitable receptacle in time. In colder countries materials such as highly absorbent moss or grass were packed into skin covers to act as nappies.

Menstrual Cloths

Folded cloths or rags have been used by a large number of different cultures as menstrual cloths, and appear to have also been used in the Roman period. A document dating to the sixth century, incorporated into a tenth-century work, describes how the mathematician and philosopher Hypatia 'gathered rags that had been stained during her period' and showed them to an over-keen admirer to put him off (Reedy 1993). In the post-Roman period there is evidence that in some sections of society women simply bled into their clothes (Finley 2006). A reference in Pliny to removing menstrual blood from clothes rather than cloths may refer to this practice, but could equally refer to simple leakage (*Natural Histories*, 27.23.85). As this method would have

1 Rebecca fetching water from a spring, represented by a nymph reclining with a water pot. She has filled a stone trough with water for the camels and offers Eliezer a drink from her pot. (*Vienna Genesis* © ÖNB/ Vienna, Cod. theol. gr. 31, p. 13)

2 Public water fountain at Pompeii. Note the stone block placed in front of the fountain to prevent damage by passing traffic, and the raised pavements and stepping stone of the side road. (© W. Griffiths)

5 Approximately 142g of raw and spun wool, with a replica wooden spindle (170mm long).

Opposite top: 3 Firewood weighing 2.7kg.

Opposite bottom: 4 Kindling. Left: soaked in olive oil (takes longer to light). Middle: covered in sulphur (burns quickly but brightly). Right: 'matches' for lighting candles and similar.

27993

27994

8 Scrubbing brush from Sedment, Egypt. (© The Trustees of the British Museum)

Opposite top: 6 Brush from Hawara, Egypt. (© UCL, Petrie Museum of Egyptian Archaeology, inventory no. UC27993)

Opposite bottom: 7 Brush from Hawara, Egypt (© UCL, Petrie Museum of Egyptian Archaeology, inventory no. UC27994)

9 Tallow candle, showing unburnt flax wick.

10 Oil lamp being filled.

11 A replica open lamp used with solid animal fat. Note how the wick has burnt along its length before dying out, while the fat at the back of the lamp remains unmelted and unburnt.

12 Detail from the kitchen scene on the Igel Monument, showing a slave drying or polishing a large dish (possible original colour scheme).

13 Detail from the kitchen scene on the Igel Monument showing dishes on the table and a slave cleaning a bowl or grinding food (possible original colour scheme).

14 Detail from the dining room scene on the Igel Monument, showing a slave to the right cleaning or polishing a serving dish (possible original colour scheme).

15 Linen after washing. Left: after wringing. Middle: hand-smoothed after wringing, which removes many but not all of the creases. Right: hand-smoothed and pressed.

16 Stone-lined drain in road at Dougga, Tunisia.

17 Tile drain pipe built into a wall, Pompeii.

18 Collecting firewood, Nepal. (© Paul Prescott)

19 Washing and drying clothes by a river, India. (© TheFinalMiracle)

20 Open drain in Jodphur, India.

involved having to wash the whole garment to remove the blood there seems to be no advantage to it when rags were easily available and involved a lot less washing, and therefore less wear and tear on expensive clothes.

Evidence suggests that Roman women did not usually wear briefs as underwear, which would have helped hold the cloths in place, but in nineteenth-century America, some women simply tucked the folded rags or pieces of sheepskin between their legs whilst in the house, and only attached the rags more securely with a belt and length of cloth when they were travelling (Anon 2006), and it is possible Roman women did the same. Menstrual cloths are usually cleaned for reuse by being soaked in cold water or, more rarely, by being boiled, although sometimes they were simply thrown away. It is not clear if the women described as 'throwing' menstrual cloths in the sea at Alexandria were trying to get rid of them or wash them (Clark 1994, 77). Menstrual blood was seen as having both good and bad qualities; on the bad side Pliny records that the ashes of menstrual blood sprinkled on to clothes being washed would rob colours of their brightness and change the shade of purple dyes, without explaining why anyone would be sprinkling the ashes on the washing in the first place (the ashes used for washing were usually alkali wood ash; *Natural Histories*, 28.23.80).

Handkerchiefs and Similar

There are a number of words for small cloths that were used for wiping sweat off the face, cleaning hands and feet after a bath (both as napkins and as cloths draped round the neck), as well as for wiping down animals and preparing food (Wild 1970b, 130–1; Suetonius, *Nero* 25, 48 and 51). Such cloths may also have been used as a handkerchief for blowing the nose, although some cultures have no need for such a cloth. A study describing the changes in attitudes to blowing one's nose in public from the fourteenth to the eighteenth centuries records a number of other methods, including closing one nostril and blowing out the other; using both fingers and throwing the mucus on to the ground before wiping the fingers on their clothes; or using a sleeve, hat or handy tablecloth as a handkerchief (Elias 1994, 117–25).

METHODS OF WASHING

Different techniques had to be used for washing linen and woollen cloth, and dyed and undyed clothes. Wools had to be treated with care to avoid further shrinkage, but linen could be treated more roughly; the usual method was to beat it to loosen the dirt from the fibres of the cloth. In the post-Roman period the cleaning of coloured or elaborate cloths usually involved the stained areas, such as under the arms or round the collar, being spot-cleaned with fuller's earth or similar before the garment was dipped in cold water to remove the dirt and smells, without any of the pounding used on the linens (Davidson 1986, 160). Where possible, dirt was simply brushed off the cloth when dry. Many of the dyes were not as fast as modern ones and could end up being washed away by the detergents along with the dirt.

Rural and Small Settlements

Cold Water, without Cleaning Agents

Roman cleaning methods on the whole involved using cold water rather than hot. The easiest method was therefore to carry the dirty laundry to the source of the water, such as a river, pond or coastal pool. This was a method that continued up until the nineteenth century as it had the advantage of constantly changing, fresh water (*ibid.*, 138–41). Sometimes large wooden tubs were also used, usually carried down to be near the water source.

Cleaning linen was not a delicate task as the cloth had to beaten vigorously to dislodge the dirt without the use of a detergent. It could be done by hand, often with the help of a wooden implement to beat it or by using the feet to pound the cloth. The choice of technique has historically been geographical rather than personal. The cloth could be rubbed or slapped against convenient stones or wooden blocks by a

Fig. 25 A professional fuller treading clothes in a tub, with a cloth draped over a beam behind him. Stone relief, from Sens, France.

Fig. 26a Professional fullers treating cloth and carrying a cage for whitening cloth. Fresco scene from an altar base, Pompeii.

Fig. 26b Washing clothes. Fresco scene from an altar base, Pompeii.

river or well, beaten against them using a ridged wooden 'beetle' or trampled by foot in a convenient pool or a wooden tub. Both techniques seem to have been used in the Roman world. Roman art shows men treading cloth in tubs (see figs 25, 26a, 26b) and Seneca mentions the 'fuller's dance' when talking about exercises that tire the body rapidly (*Letters*, 15.4), while the story of the death of St James records that he was killed by a fuller using 'the club with which he beat out clothes' (Eusebius, *History of the Church*, 2.23.18).

Pliny, when talking about the many uses of seawater, mentions that it also softens wool, and he goes on to explain how to make saltwater when not living by the coast (*Natural Histories*, 31.33.66). In contrast, Plutarch suggested the topic of 'why fresh water instead of seawater is used to wash clothes' as one of his themes for discussion round the dinner table. One speaker, Theon, suggested that as river water had a 'light consistency', it could soak through the cloth and dissolve the dirt better than the more 'earthy' saltwater. Plutarch himself put forward two theories: he argued that as 'everything oily is hard to wash and makes a stain', seawater could not be an efficient cleanser since it was oily itself, and then observed that as whatever dried fastest looked cleanest, fresh water dried faster than saltwater 'since its coarseness holds it in the mesh of the cloth' (*Moralia, Table-talk* 7, question 9).

Cold Water, with Cleaning Agents

It was easier to clean clothes using simple detergents such as mud, lye or urine in a container. In the Roman period professional fullers sometimes made use of wooden tubs (see fig. 25), so it is probable that they were also used in domestic settings. They could either be carried to the water supply for use there, or else used in or near the house, although this involved much more effort as the tub had to be constantly filled with water carried up from the water source, emptied and refilled.

Even with detergent added to the water, the clothes still needed to be beaten and pounded, although not for as long as was needed when washing without detergent. A major drawback to using cold water was that as washing had to be done all the year round, the legs and arms of those doing the work could suffer badly; the post-Roman period observers refer to women's legs being swollen black and blue or blood red as a result of washing in cold water (Davidson 1986, 138–40).

Hot Water

Hot water can make clothes fade and shrink, but is useful for dealing with heavily soiled cloths. In the Roman period washing in hot water was probably restricted to undyed linens. Pliny mentions linen being boiled, warning that the touch of a menstruating woman would turn it black (*Natural Histories*, 28.23.79). Hot water would also be required when washing with soap or soapwort. Washing with hot water would have been carried out inside the house, either by pouring hot water into a wooden tub (probably set on a stool or table) or by boiling clothes in metal containers suspended over the fire.

Cities

The rich, owning houses with piped water and large peristyles or gardens that could be used for drying, may well have been in a position to do their own washing, but for the poor living in crowded tenements it was a different matter. Water may have been carried back to wooden tubs for indoor use or public water resources such as rivers may have been used. Hellenistic-period regulations at Pergamum decreed that people could not wash clothes in public fountains under threat of losing the clothes and being fined, and it seems likely there were similar rules in the Roman period to stop the contamination of what was meant as drinking water (Liebeshuetz 2000, 57–8). Although washing clothes in public fountains in the Mediterranean region may have been forbidden, it was possibly different in other provinces. The water tank at the end of the aqueduct leading into Corbridge Roman town has scalloped edges, which has been identified as wear from the rubbing of clothes against the tank wall (Johnston 1978, 175). Water tanks inside the fort at Housesteads also have similar worn edges (Crow 2004, figs 20, 23).

Drying the clothes would be even more difficult than washing them, as the law stated that only fullers were allowed to hang clothes to dry out in the streets (*Digest*, 43.10.1.4). This law was either disregarded or else the laundry had to be hung up inside to dry (as on wet days), with all the drawbacks of the lack of space and dripping clothes to endure. In more recent times, putting up with the laundry drying inside on wet days was often considered the worse part of wash days.

Fullers

In cities it may have been more common to send the laundry out to professional fullers, although this meant paying for the service. Fullers had two separate roles, one finishing new cloth straight from the loom and the other cleaning already worn clothes. Finishing involved carrying out the initial shrinking of woollen cloth, making the clothes wearable by removing the natural greases and finishing the surface treatment such as raising the nap or smoothing the cloth. Diocletian's *Edict of Maximum Prices* includes different prices for the fullers to prepare unfinished (*rudis*) clothes and to wash those that had already been 'polished' or finished (*levis*; Bradley 2002, 21–2), although it is not clear whether the same establishment carried out both roles, or whether individual businesses specialised in one or the other.

Fulling establishments needed a good water supply, masonry tanks or wooden tubs for treading and rinsing, and space to dry the clothes. Cloth was an expensive commodity in the ancient world, and fulleries were important businesses within cities; those in Pompeii and Ostia were set up in converted houses near to some of the most important buildings in the towns, while Antioch built a special aqueduct just to supply water to them (Bradley 2002, 36, 38). Wall paintings from Pompeii and reliefs from France show the stages involved in fulling: men are shown standing in circular or rectangular tubs or tanks, which are often provided with handrails to stop them slipping, pounding the cloth with their feet (see figs 25, 26a, 26b). Other men are shown rinsing the clothes in similar tubs. The clothes were then hung over wooden beams suspended from the ceiling to dry (see figs 25, 29; Robertson 1986, fig. 13).

CLEANING AGENTS

A surprising number of different agents are recorded as having been used to finish or clean cloth. Sometimes the choice of what to use must have been a matter of personal preference, but there were no doubt strong regional variations according to both the availability of the cleaning agents and what was traditional in any given area.

Urine

The Romans used urine extensively in cleaning clothes. Isidore records that it was 'called "piss" (*lotium*) by the common people because with its help clothes were washed (*lotus*), that is, cleaned' (*Etymologies*, 11.1.138, trans. Barney *et al.* 2006). Professional fullers, who required large quantities of the stuff, set up jars in the streets to collect urine from passers-by, and also collected it from public toilets in bathhouses (Bradley 2002, 30). At a household level, it was a free commodity that could easily be acquired and kept until needed; as late as the 1930s households in the Hebrides still kept it in tubs to finish the home-spun and -woven tweeds being produced by the families (MacDonald 1982, 20–1).

    Stale urine was used because of its ammonia content, and the longer it had been kept, the more potent it became. Its advantage is that a chemical transformation takes place when it combines with grease, creating a soap-like substance (Bradley 2002, 30). As well as being a cleansing agent, it was also used to full cloth straight from the loom, as part of the finishing process. Urine was recommended for removing ink spots and stains of menstrual blood on clothes (although it had to be that of the same woman; Pliny, *Natural Histories*, 28.18.66, 27.23). Clothes, when either fulled with urine or washed with urine, continued to smell even after rinsing (Bradley 2002, 36; MacDonald 1982, 20), but to a Roman this was simply a welcome indication of new or cleaned clothes.

Fuller's Earth

Fuller's earth is the term used for calcium montmorillonite, a strongly absorbent earth that when rubbed on to cloth absorbs greasy residues which can then be rinsed away. It has been used throughout history for fulling new woollen cloth, and was probably also used to launder clothes. True fuller's earth is only available in certain geographical areas, although in other areas less effective earths may have been used instead. Unlike urine with its universal availability, the use of fuller's earth would have been more regional. In Britain, for example, it is mainly found in the south of the country. Fuller's earth is said to have been found in a timber-lined pit at Chichester, but it was not tested (Robertson 1986, 81). Some fuller's earth may have been traded outside its immediate area; Pliny talks about the earths from Cimolia, Sardinia and Umbria and their different properties, and some fuller's earth found at Pompeii may have come from Ponza, on the Pontine Islands off the coast of Italy halfway between Rome and Naples (*ibid.*, 52).

Fuller's earth had to be used with some care, as it could affect coloured dyes, and even remove them altogether. Pliny notes that Sardinian earth was good for white cloth, but not for coloured cloths, while Cimolian earth could be used to brighten up 'genuine and valuable' colours, but could turn some cheap dyes black (*Natural Histories*, 35.57.198).

Ash and Soda

Plutarch notes:

> people frequently thicken their water with ash, or soda, or if these are not at hand, with a powdery solid; the earthy matter, it would seem, is more easily able by its roughness to wash out dirt while the water alone, because of its lightness and weakness, does not do this with equal facility. (*Moralia, Table-talk*, question 9)

The 'powdery solids' were presumably different types of mud or minerals. Both wood ash (also used in producing lye) and soda are alkali, so when grease comes in contact with them it becomes more soluble in water and can be washed away. The soda (sodium carbonate) could be collected as a natural mineral found near the remains of saline lake beds or could be recovered by burning seaweed or salt-tolerant plants such as glassworts and saltworts. The ashes of the plants were soaked in water, which was then boiled to form 'soda ash' or 'washing soda' and was even more alkali than wood ash (which contained potassium rather than sodium: Robertson 1986, 23).

Sodium carbonate is a major component of natron, a naturally occurring mix which also includes sodium bicarbonate, salt and sodium sulphate, and was also used as a detergent. Isidore records it as being used for making medicines and to wash 'dirty clothes and bodies' (*Etymologies*, 16.2.7, trans. Barney *et al.* 2006), while Soranus recommends that care should be taken that the bandages used for swaddling babies should be clean, not evil-smelling and should not irritate the skin by containing natron (*Gynecology*, 2.14[83], trans. Temkin 1956).

Soapwort

Soapwort was used to clean the natural grease out of raw wool before dying and spinning; Isidore recorded that the plant was sometimes called the 'woolworkers' plant' because they washed wool with it (*Etymologies*, 17.9.56, trans. Barney *et al.* 2006; *Stockholm Papyrus* 97, 102, 106, 115, 122, trans. Caley 1926b). It is probable that the plant called 'rootlet' by Pliny was also soapwort; he describes it as having a 'juice that is only used for washing wool, contributing in a remarkable degree to its whiteness and softness' (*Natural Histories*, 19.28.48). As Dioscorides mentions that it was used by fullers, it is likely it was also used on finished cloth as well as on raw wool (*On Medical Matters*, 2.193).

Soapwort, a member of the carnation family, is rich in saponins, which produce a lather when mixed with water. The leaves and roots were crushed and added to the water to create a mild detergent. A recipe in the *Stockholm Papyrus* explains the method: 'Cleaning with soapwort is done in the following way: take and bruise soapwort, put it in water and heat it. Then put the wool in and shake it a little. Lift out and dry.' A second recipe recommends:

> Take and treat soapwort with hot water. Make a ball from it as if from tallow. Then steep this in hot water until it is dissolved ... Then boil up the water. Put the wool in and prevent it from being scorched. Leave it there a little while until you can see that it is clean. Lift out, rinse it and dry it. (85, 145, trans. Caley 1926b)

Soap

In the Roman world soap, made of fat and wood ash, is described as being used as hair dye (Pliny, *Natural Histories*, 28.12.191) or 'for washing the head' and as a medicine (such as removing bruises or lividity from the face: Partington and Hall 1999, 306–7; Serenus, *Book of Medicine* 11.153). Galen, however, seems to refer to 'true' soap made with causticised lye, used to remove impurities from clothes as well as the body, saying that it was a better detergent than soda (Partington and Hall 1999, 307). In Diocletian's *Edict of Maximum Prices* it was priced at 100 *denarii* for 1lb (32.33).

From early times soap was an expensive commodity as it was made with animal fat that could also be put to other uses, such as cooking or candle-making. For many centuries, soap and lye were used together, and it was not until the second half of the eighteenth century that soap was used exclusively for washing clothes (Davidson 1986, 144).

Lye

In the post-Roman period lye was frequently used to remove dirt from clothes, and as the Romans knew how to make lye for cleaning pottery vessels, it may have also been used by them as a detergent in cleaning clothes.

Other

The lees of wine that had lost their strength could be used to clean woollen cloth, being 'useful for washing the person as well as clothes; for this purpose they take the place of gum arabic' (Pliny *Natural Histories*, 23.32.65). Gum arabic is the gum of the acacia trees of Africa, and when dissolved in water reduces surface tensions in liquids, increases viscosity and improves flow, and helps suspend other additions to the liquid. In terms of washing clothes, in more recent times it was typically used to add some stiffness to fine cloths.

DRYING

After the cloths had been washed, they needed to be wrung out. There is no evidence whether the Romans wrung out their laundry simply by hand or by folding it round an upright post before twisting to get as much water out as possible, as depicted in ancient Egyptian art (and possibly also in Greek art, such as in a scene on a vase where a woman holding a wrung cloth stands next to a slight-waisted stone or timber that may have been used in the same way: Robertson 1986, figs 2 and 5; cf. fig. 27). Greek art shows women wringing clothes by twisting them while one end is held firm between their legs (see fig. 27).

After being wrung out the laundry had to be dried, and the same Greek vase painting, illustrating the story of Ulysses meeting Nausicca and her companions while they do their laundry, shows the clothes hanging to dry on the branches of a tree (see fig. 27), although Homer's version of the story describes the women laying the clothes out to dry on the ground (Robertson 1986, 7, fig. 2).

Both of these methods were also used in the post-Roman period: it was usual, in those areas where there was plenty of available space out in the country or on the outskirts of towns, to lay the laundry on the ground, draped over hedges and tree branches, or placed over poles held between two forked uprights (Davidson 1986, figs 85, 92; Filbee 1980, 74). Large country houses often had large bushes planted nearby for exactly this purpose, and in 1613 Gervase Markham suggests knot gardens should have borders of privet or box 18in wide and with cropped flat tops as they were both ornamental and could be used for the 'drying of linen clothes, yarn and such like' (Markham 1613, chapter 17). A map of *c.*1559 of London shows a large field,

Fig. 27a–b Greek women wringing laundry. a: Attic red figure amphora, Munich 2322 (Antikensammlungen und Glyptothek, Munich); b: from pyxis lid by the painter Aison (Museum of Fine Arts, Boston).

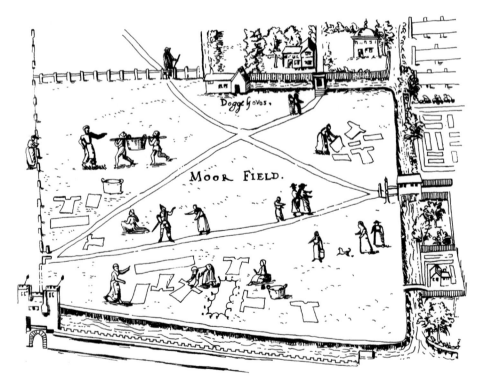

Fig. 28 Map of Moorfields, London, dated c.1559, showing clothes being laid out to dry.

Moorfields, inside the city walls, where people have laid out their laundry to dry (see fig. 28). The drawbacks to laying laundry out on the ground were the need for a dry surface underfoot, having to pin clothes down with stones to stop them flapping about on windy days, keeping muddy-footed animals and young children from running across them and the necessity of having someone watching over the laundry to avoid losing it to thieves when it was laid out in public spaces.

Where specially built structures were used to carry the clothes, it would appear the laundry was usually hung over wooden poles suspended from the ceiling inside. While the clothes line seems to have been known, it does not appear to have been widely used, and was possibly restricted to houses and gardens within large cities where there was little available space for laying out on the ground. There is no evidence for the use of clothes pegs. A clothes line is mentioned in a fourth-century letter written by Sidonius, in a story about a group of churchmen who retired to the Tomb of Syagrius in Lyons whilst waiting between church services. At first they sat under a vine or on the grass and talked, but they then split up between those who played board games and those involved in an energetic ball game. One exhausted man had to retire early from the game and:

> the pouring sweat next prompted him to ask for water to bathe his face. It was brought at his request, along with a thick shaggy towel which, by chance, had been cleaned of the previous day's dirt, and was swinging on a rope belonging to the porter which had been raised by a pulley close to the double folding doors of the small building. (*Letters*, 5.17.8)

When two guests fell into a fishpond in a rich man's house and went to the baths to clean themselves during Trimalchio's meal, as recorded in Petronius' novel, their slave dried their clothes 'in the entrance', although it is not clear if this is the entrance to the bath suite or the whole house (*Satyricon*, 73), nor how he dried them.

WHITENING

Laying linens out in the sun to dry would have helped bleach them, but for some clothes a purer white was required. There were two methods of doing this: one, probably only done by professional fullers, was to drape clothes over a semi-circular wickerwork frame and fumigate them by burning sulphur underneath. A wall painting from Pompeii shows a man carrying such a frame (see fig. 26), and in Apuleius' *Metamorphoses* a lover tries to hide from a jealous husband under such a frame, but the strong fumes of the sulphur start him sneezing (9.24). The clothes naturally smelt of sulphur at the end of the treatment and had a tendency to turn yellowish in time.

The other, simpler method was to impregnate the cloth with fine particles of white pigment to create a brilliant white. Chalk, kaolin and lime all seem to have been used to make clothes white (Bradley 2002, 29; Robertson 1986, 55).

SMOOTHING

The damp clothes or cloths were almost certainly smoothed by hand as far as possible before being laid out to dry in order to reduce the number of creases (see plate 15). In later periods linen was sometimes beaten and polished both to flatten the seams and to produce a smooth and glossy surface (Walton Rogers 1997, 1775). In the post-Roman period, this smoothing was carried out using objects called 'linen-smoothers' or 'slick-stones', which were circular, slightly domed glass or stone discs that were rubbed across the cloth while it was stretched over a suitable flat surface. The lower face of a typical linen-smoother has a slightly dull face, with microscopic scratch marks on it whose direction suggest a back-and-forth action rather than a circular movement (*ibid.*, fig. 828).

A small number of objects from Roman sites have been identified as possible linen-smoothers. There are two from Britain, both unstratified, from the vicinity of South Shields Roman fort, but these are half the size of the later examples and, being almost spherical, have only a very small smoothing surface (Wild 1970a, fig. 76). Another, from a certain Roman context, from Hees near Nijmegen, is much larger and may be a more likely example (*ibid.*, 85). Stone examples made from natural smooth pebbles, which could easily be overlooked in the archaeological record, may also have been used.

In the nineteenth century Chinese laundrymen would dampen clothes before ironing by taking a mouthful of water and spraying it over the cloth (Bowles 1866, letter 23; Wai-Ma 1984, 33). This method was also apparently used in the Roman period, as described by Seneca when explaining rainbows:

> Watch a fuller, if you like, and you will see the same thing happen sometimes …
> When he fills his mouth with water and gently sprays it on clothes spread out
> on stretchers it appears as though the various colours which usually shine in a
> rainbow are produced in that sprayed air. (*Natural Questions*, 1.3.2)

In this case instead of using a hot iron to smooth away creases, the clothes referred to were either stretched over a frame or were wrapped round boards before being put into a screw press (see fig. 29a).

Using a screw press involved placing the folded cloths on a solid wooden board while a second, upper, board was screwed down tightly on to them. A complete

Fig. 29a A clothespress in a fullery. Fresco scene from an altar base, Pompeii.

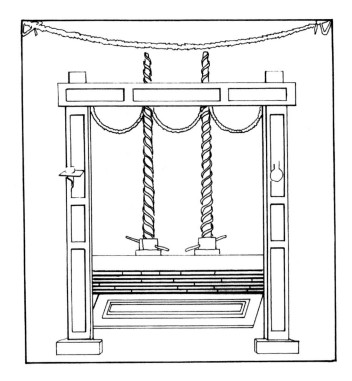

Fig. 29b Clothes hanging from wooden poles. Fresco scene from an altar base, Pompeii.

wooden single-screw press survives from Herculaneum and the iron fittings of a two-screw example were found at Pompeii. A reconstruction of the two-screw press, based on the famous wall painting of such a press from a fullery (VI, 8, 20), was given a board 1.7m long and 0.5m wide, although Forbes has suggested a 'typical' size was 0.6m x 0.45m (Spinazzola 1953, figs 764–6; Forbes 1955, 137; see fig. 29).

The Pompeian fittings and the wall painting were associated with professional fulleries, but that from Herculaneum does not appear to have been. While they were no doubt more common in commercial establishments, some were probably also used in the private houses of the rich. Authors refer to clothes being taken out of presses after bathing, and mention silken clothes belonging to the Empress and multiple cloaks in the press of a rich man, suggesting that clothes could be stored in them (Claudian, *Epithalamium of Palladius and Celerina*, 101; Martial, *Epigrams*, 2.46.3, 11.8.5); however, in an unflattering account of a rich man who had brought an unnecessarily large choice of clothing to change into after bathing, the press is clearly portable, and something other than a screw press must be intended (Ammianus Marcellinus, *Roman History*, 28.4.19). It is possible the presses used to store clothes were not the same as those used to smooth them; in the post-medieval period the term 'linen-press' could mean both a screw press and a cupboard with shallow shelves where the pressed items were stored before use, and it may have been the same in the Roman period.

A more usual way of bringing fresh clothes to the baths was for a slave to carry them in a shallow, open-topped box. Scenes of processions towards the bath often show the boxes being carried, and a mosaic from the villa at Piazza Armerina of a man getting dried after a bath shows a slave presenting him with a neatly folded clean tunic (Croom 2000, pl. 8; Croom 2007, figs 50, 71). It is not clear if the shallow boxes were ever used for storing clothes or were just for transporting them.

The clothespress was probably originally designed to help flatten cloth, but in time it may have come to be used principally to add creases to it. Neat fold marks in clothes would have emphasised the fact that they were either brand new or were just newly laundered, and so may have become a status symbol (Grainger-Taylor 1987, 122). Such fold lines are occasionally represented on statues, but they require some skill to depict and were probably much more common in real life than Roman art would suggest. While clean and pressed clothes might be an indication of wealth, for some they brought their own problems. Seneca complained: 'I do not like … a garment brought from a small chest, nor one pressed by weights and a thousand tortures to force it to be bright, but a house-garment of little value, that has neither been watched over or selected with care' (*On Tranquillity of Mind*, 1.5).

Clothes and cloth furnishings were generally stored in chests or cupboards (cf. Dioscorides, *On Medical Matters*, 1.166, Horace, *Satires*, 2.3.119; Croom 2007, 127–8; a fragment of woollen textile from Pompeii that had at least 20 aligned layers: Grainger-Taylor 1987, 120). Similar fold lines to those produced by a press can be created, if less effectively but more cheaply, by carefully storing folded textiles in chests, or squeezed between shelves in a cupboard. This relies on the weight of the upper textiles pressing down on the lowest ones, with a little added pressure from the chest lid or an upper shelf in the cupboard.

Another method of smoothing cloth and producing folds is the use of 'ironing sticks', as used in Korea and Japan: the folded clothes are placed on a smooth rectangular stone or wooden board and then beaten with rounded sticks for some time (see two photographs in the Corwin and Nellie Taylor collection: www.usc.edu/libraries/archives/arc/libraries/eastasian/korea/resources/kda-taylor2.html). There is no evidence that this method was used in the Roman period, but it is a simple and effective method that would leave little traces in the archaeological record, and there may have been a number of different traditional methods used across the empire.

MAINTENANCE

Linen clothes in particular crease easily on being worn, and it seems likely that the Romans had some way of smoothing out the worst creases in between washings. In very rich households presses could be used and there were slaves who specialised in folding and putting away clothes, probably under the direction of a higher-ranking slave who had overall responsibility for looking after the clothes (Treggiari 1976, 80). The less rich might just have had to hope that careful folding and storage would work, but it is likely Romans looked a lot more crumpled than modern tastes would accept.

10

DISPOSAL:
WASTE WATER AND SEWAGE

In modern terminology, the word 'sewer' is used to describe a conduit for the removal of human waste, while a 'drain' is for rainwater and other run-offs. In the Roman period there was no such distinction, with sewage often thrown out into street drains and the overflow from fountains feeding into sewers. In the following account, 'sewer' is used to mean a below-ground conduit that was buried and hidden, whilst 'drain' is used for ground-level conduits that were either open or partially covered by stone slabs (see plate 16).

The large underground sewers were usually only to be found in large towns or cities. They were not built principally for the health of the inhabitants but because the large amount of sewage produced daily had to be removed one way or another, and sewers were the quickest and easiest method of doing it. Underground sewers were usually built at the same time as the road above them, rather than being inserted into existing roads, but existing drains, or streams used as drains, could be converted into sewers (Hodge 1992, 340). Pliny asked the Emperor Trajan for permission for just such an operation:

Among the chief features of Amastris ... a city which is well built and laid out, is a long street of great beauty. Through-out the length of it, however, there runs what is called a stream, but is in fact a filthy drain, a disgusting eyesore which gives off a noxious stench. The health and appearance alike of the city will benefit if it is covered in. (*Letters*, 10.98)

Branch pipelines and drains from individual buildings or side streets fed into the main sewer, while simple holes took waste directly from the street. Some roads had openings in the vertical face of pavement curb stones (sometimes with a metal grid to keep out debris), while others had stone gratings set into the road surface cut with petal-shaped openings (Hodge 1992, 340–1).

The public fountains were supplied with a constant flow of water, so whenever water collection from the tank did not keep the level sufficiently low, the excess would flow out of the tank and into the street (as would have happened throughout the night). This overflow was an intentional part of the water supply system. Frontinus quotes an official decree stating that: 'an overflow from the secondary water towers is vital, for this is used not only to keep the city healthy but also to the practical end of scouring out the sewer' (*On Aqueducts*, 2.111). The overflow simply followed the lie of the land, washing away any waste in its way, and eventually drained into a sewer.

Planned settlements such as new colonies or military camps were designed to have a network of drains down the middle of many of their roads. At Timgad, the newly built colony was designed with underground sewers in the side streets leading to larger collectors under the main roads (Wilson 2000, 307). However, even those towns and cities that had sewers and drains built in some sections of the settlement often also had sections, sometimes large, which had neither, and the waste water just followed the lie of the ground surface (Hodge 1992, 334). Drains could sometimes be flushed by the overflow from fountains or from bath suites, but if they relied purely on the run-off from rain, then the drains would only be flushed intermittently. The drains were usually made of stone slabs which had plenty of edges and rough surfaces to catch and impede the progress of any solids within the drain so they were likely to smell, as Pliny noted at Amastris. Solids which had settled to the bottom would also need to be periodically cleaned out, an operation which was sometimes the responsibility of city officials and sometimes that of the owners of the neighbouring shops (Wilson 2000, 307).

Where possible, the main sewer or drain eventually discharged into a river to disperse the waste. It is also possible that in some places sewers were left to drain their contents over a large area of ground on a 'soakaway system' where, as the name indicates, the contents just soaked into the ground (Hodge 1992, 343). At Bearsden fort, the outflow of the bath house latrine simply fed into the ditches immediately outside the wall. Deposits in the outer ditch contained plant remains and intestinal parasites suggestive of human faecal material, while the insect remains indicate the presence of rotting organic material and very shallow, stagnant water (Knights *et al.* 1983, 143–4).

The methods used to get rid of waste water and sewage would have varied from town to town, according to the nature of the subsoil and the gradient of the land. At Ostia, for example, there was only a 2.5m difference between the highest and lowest points, so the town officials preferred to use a sewer system rather than rely on the water flowing along the street surfaces; at Pompeii a porous subsoil meant that the fill of cesspits could be easily absorbed, while the hard subsoil at Herculaneum would have meant cesspits had to be emptied by hand (Jansen 2000a, 45–7, 38, 43). Settlements without aqueducts to bring in a constant supply of water to fountains had to rely on rain water to flush out the drains.

WASTE WATER

Households would produce waste liquids on a daily basis. Much of the waste came from the kitchen, left over from preparing food and cooking as well as the used washing-up water, but there was also dirty water from the washing of hands (and sometimes feet) in the dining room and from washing in basins in bedrooms, plus water used to clean the floors.

Rural Settlements and Villas

In rural settlements water could simply be thrown out to soak into the ground without walking too far away from the house. It could be poured into nearby vegetable gardens, on to waste ground, into ditches or simply on to metalling such as yards and paths. If the water is not constantly thrown away on the same patch it can usually soakaway easily and does not cause problems.

Towns and Forts

In larger settlements the quantity of water involved meant there had to be some form of drainage to remove the water from the immediate vicinity of the buildings to avoid constant puddles. In more sophisticated houses there would sometimes be stone-lined drains leading outside so that water could be disposed of from within the house, although the efficiency of the system depended on the gradient of the drain. In Silchester some of the rooms with mosaics had small drains made from curved roofing tiles set into the wall to drain away the water used in washing the floor (Boon 1957, 155), and the water tanks of *atrium*-type houses often had drains leading out to the street to avoid overflowing tanks flooding the room (Hobson 2009, fig. 120). In Pompeii and Herculaneum some kitchen drains simply channelled the liquid waste directly into the street, where it might be washed away by the running water from the public fountains. Waste water could also be thrown into pit latrines, where the liquid would percolate into the surrounding soil.

In houses without drains, water would have been thrown out by hand, which usually meant simply out into the street outside the building. Military establishments were built with drains down the centre of their roads which served to carry away rain water as well as waste water and so avoid constantly muddy streets. The water in such drains could also be used to flush out the multi-seater latrines, as in the Roman fort at Housesteads, where road drains led down to the latrine building which had been deliberately positioned in the lowest corner of the fort. In this case, water could also be channelled through the latrines from a number of open cisterns built nearby. The overflow from the largest cistern, which could hold approximately 24,000 litres, was also directed through the latrine (Crow 2004, 41–4, figs 21–3).

In larger towns with paved roads, the water would either find its way into the central stone-lined drains or stay on the street surface and simply flow downhill under gravity. All such waste water would have helped to wash away any sewage lying in the street, and with the overflow from public fountains, some streets in the larger towns must have been almost constantly wet. Some of the streets in Pompeii have raised pavements and stepping stones across the street, so that people could avoid the water and dirt of the street itself (see plate 2). In some towns without proper drains, such as Berenice in Africa, waste water from private houses was discharged into soakaway pits in the streets, although this system was more usual when dealing with large quantities of water from baths or industrial processes (Wilson 2000, 308–9).

Cities

In the houses of the rich which had pipe drains leading to town sewers, the water could be quickly removed from the house. In some houses with mosaic floors a special drain could be built into dining rooms: 'It has been held that a hole at the bottom of a wall of a private chamber or dining-room, designed for washing the floor, does not imply a right to discharge a constant flow of water' (*Digest*, 8.2.28; as seen at Silchester), but in most houses a single central drain would have been more usual.

House owners were responsible for making sure their drains were in good condition, as discussed in a section dealing with 'drains' in Roman law books:

2. The praetor has taken care [by this ruling] for the cleaning and the repair of drains. Both pertain to the health of the city and to safety. For drains choked with filth threaten pestilence of the atmosphere and ruin, if they are not repaired.
3. This interdict is provided for private drains, as public drains deserve public care.
4. A drain is a hollow place through which certain waste liquids should flow …
6. Under the term 'drain' are included tubes and pipes …
9. Pomponius also writes that if anyone wishes to make a drain so that it has an outlet into the public drain, he is not to be hindered.

(*Digest of Justinian*, 43.23)

In houses or apartments without the refinements of drains or pit latrines, the water could be thrown out of any convenient door or the windows of upper storeys. When Juvenal complains of the crowded streets of Rome, he observed: 'You should pray and carry with you this pitiable wish: that people may be content to empty over you, from their windows, only an open basin [i.e. of dirty water, not the contents of a chamber pot]' (*Satires*, 3, 276–7).

SEWAGE DISPOSAL

Open Defecation

'Open defecation' is the term used for the practice of defecating wherever it is convenient, such as in fields, by the side of the road and under trees. It works best in small rural communities, where there are numerous suitable places in the area. It has a number of advantages: it avoids the smells and flies often associated with cesspits inside buildings; the faeces dry quickly in hot weather and therefore do not smell; and it acts as fertilizer in the field; in addition, in some situations it also has social advantages such as giving women an opportunity to get out of the house and meet up with friends (Pickford 1995, 22; Khanna and Khanna 2006, 30–1). The disadvantages of the system include the lack of shelter in wet or cold weather, the difficulty of going out in the dark at night, a lack of privacy (a special concern for women) and sometimes a long walk from the centre of a village to find a suitable location (Pickford 1995, 21, 24).

Open defecation also takes place in towns and cities, where it is more problematic due to the lack of suitable open spaces and a much larger population and correspondingly larger volume of waste. In the medieval period and later, alleys and side streets were much used. Nor did defecation happen only outside: in establishments with a large number of people the inhabitants, particularly visitors, did not always bother to find chamber pots or privies even if provided. The 1589 Court Regulations of Brunswick include the ruling that 'no one, whoever he may be, before, at, or after meals, early or late, foul the corridors or closets with urine or other filth', while when the court of Charles II visited Oxford in 1660, it was reported that on their departure they left 'their excrements in every corner, in chimneys, studies, coal-houses, cellars', and even the corridors and courtyards at Versailles suffered similarly (Elias 1994, 107; Picard 2001a, 14; Spawforth 2008, 151–2). That this practice might also have occurred inside Roman houses is suggested by house leases from Egypt that often specify that rooms should be 'cleansed of excrements and every kind of filth' before the end of the contract (Parsons 2007, 54).

Open defecation must have been used extensively in the Roman world, both in the countryside and in towns and cities. The nooks and crannies of the large tombs lining the roads out of settlements in particular were attractive locations for people wanting to relieve themselves, and those who owned or looked after the tombs sometimes set up signs warning against it. A graffito from Pompeii on a tomb outside the Porta Vesuvio pleads: 'if you wish to shit, move away from this place' (see fig. 30; *CIL* 4, no 6641), and when the fictional character Trimalchio describes the tomb he wants erected for himself he specifies that: 'I am appointing one of the freedmen to be caretaker of the tomb so that the common people won't run up and shit near it' (Petronius, *Satyricon*, 71). The tomb of Julia Fericula and Evaristus in Rome also refers to the problem: 'Passer-by, do not make water on this tomb, the bones of the man buried here beg you. If you are an agreeable man, drink and give to me a mixed drink [of water and wine]' (*CIL* 6, no 2357). The phrase was common enough on tombstones to be parodied on a graffito written on a building in Pompeii: 'Passer-by, do not piss on this tomb, the bones beg, nor shit, if you are even more obliging. You see here the tomb of Urtica [= Nettle]. Go away, shitter, it is not safe to open your bowels here' (*CIL* 4, no 8899).

Graffiti from Pompeii shows it was also a concern within the town itself as there are a number of scratched messages on walls all with the basic theme of 'do not defecate here', but with a bit more force to back up the order: 'whoever shits [here], beware of bad luck' (*CIL* 4, nos 3782, 3832, 4586, 5438). An extended version, written on the wall by the door to the House of Pascius Hermes, involves the gods: 'who shits [here], beware of bad luck. Jupiter's anger if you scorn this' (*CIL* 4, no 7716; a relief from Aquileia in Italy apparently shows a man who has ignored the warnings about to suffer Jupiter's anger: Wilson 2000, fig. 4). At Thigibba in Africa it was felt necessary to include an inscription on the base of an honorific arch that probably led into the forum itself, reading: 'anybody urinating here will incur the wrath of Mars' (*ibid.*, 310).

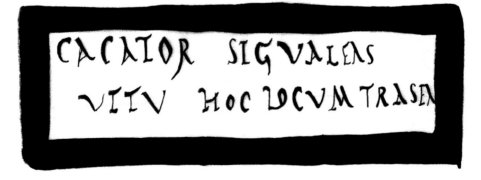

Fig. 30 Painted sign reading 'If you wish to shit, move away from this place', from Pompeii, tomb outside Porta Vesuvio.

Human faecal material found during excavations at York also provides some evidence for open defecation (Hall *et al.* 1990, 391). The area under excavation was situated in the *colonia* a few metres away from one of the main roads leading out of the fortress, which seems to have been largely empty and used periodically for dumping rubbish from elsewhere. The faecal material was found not only in drains but in the fills of cut features, as if there had been a preference for pits or similar depressions in the landscape when the people relieved themselves.

Inside the house

Chamber Pots

In the medieval period pottery urinals, and in the post-medieval period pottery chamber pots, were made in forms that were not used for any other purpose, and the use of a purposely designed vessel continued up until the twentieth century. No such vessel has been identified in Romano-British pottery, so it is likely that people used whatever they felt was suitable, as happened elsewhere in the empire. Martial records an incident where a flagon that had held wine from the town of Spoleto was used: 'When the drunk Panaretus snapped this thumb for a chamber-pot in the middle of the night he was handed a Spoletine flagon, one that he had drained himself' (Martial, *Epigrams*, 6.89).

Literary sources generally refer to chamber pots made of metal, which was perhaps preferred to pottery as it was easier to clean effectively. Some were made of bronze, and a number of authors made the most of the irony that they could be made from the reused statues of the great and good (Martial, *Epigrams*, 14.119; Juvenal, *Satires*, 10.64). Most references are to examples made in more expensive materials, but this is simply because the authors were scornful of the extravagance and could make much of the contrast between the costly material used for the container and the unpleasant nature of its contents. The Emperor Elagabalus had examples of gold and stone ones carved out of murra and onyx (*SHA Elagabalus,* 32.2), while the Christian writer Clement of Alexandria thought it 'a distinctly ridiculous matter, deserving of the maximum derision, for men to bring forward silver urinal vessels and glass chamber-pots ... and for rich women without sense to have vessels made out of gold for excrement' (*The Instructor*, 2.3; cf. *Digest*, 34.27.5; Martial, *Epigrams*, 1.37). The literary evidence indicates that one type of chamber pot was called 'boat-shaped', but otherwise nothing is known of the form these vessels took.

A guest expected one to be available in his room, as indicated by a graffito by the entrance to a house in Pompeii: 'Dear host, I'm afraid I've wet the bed. "Why?" you ask. Because there was no chamber-pot in my room' (*CIL* 4, no 4957). Martial's gift tag for a chamber pot has a similar theme: 'When I [i.e. the chamber pot] am summoned with a snap of the fingers and the slave delays, oh how often has the mattress become my rival' (Martial, *Epigrams*, 14.119).

A chamber-pot has the advantage of being suitable for use in whichever room in the house was most convenient. In 1664, a rich noblewoman caught short whilst out and about nipped into the house of her friends the Pepys and was using a chamber pot in the dining room when Pepys, unaware of the reason for her visit and anxious to show her respect, barged in and proceeded to hold a very embarrassed conversation with her (Picard 2001a, 40). Dining rooms have often been the repository for chamber pots, so that men did not have to leave the room to relieve themselves, and as late as the nineteenth century the rich commissioned expensive sideboards (commodes) to hold the pots as an integral part of their dining room furniture.

Trimalchio used a chamber pot in the bathhouse, and in his house kept chamber pots either in the corridor or a room near his dining room:

> After this course Trimalchio rose to go to the pot. With the tyrant away we had our freedom and we proceeded to draw the conversation of our neighbours ... Gossip was in the air, when Trimalchio came in mopping his brow and washed his hands in scent. [After talk of the state of his bowels he offered the facilities to his guests, adding:] 'If the matter is serious, everything is ready outside: water, chamber-pots and all the other trifles'. (Petronius, *Satyricon*, 41; 47)

Slave or family members would have had to empty the chamber pots on a regular basis, either taking them away immediately after they had been used or collecting those used at night first thing in the morning. Where they emptied the contents depended on the facilities available elsewhere in the house: they could be emptied into a pit latrine within the house, into a pipe drain leading to a sewer or else simply straight out of the door on to the street, which may or may not have had an open drain running down it. Some houses in Pompeii have vertical pipe drains made of interlocking clay pipes built into the wall leading down from niche latrines in the upper stories (see plate 17, fig. 31), which

Fig. 31 Cross-section through an upper-storey niche toilet, showing the niche and the pipe made up of interlocking tile sections set into the wall. (After Jansen 1997)

were used for getting rid of sewage and waste water (the waste water would help wash the sewage away, and hopefully keep the smell down, as the lack of a U-bend meant any conduit leading to a sewer would end up smelling badly). It is assumed the pipes lead to a cesspit, a sewer or simply empty out on to the street, although this has seldom been proved by excavation. People living in the upper storeys of tenements without such pipe drains almost certainly frequently emptied chamber pots out of the window.

Toilets

As in many pre-industrial societies, the Romans did not expect total privacy when going to the toilet outside their home. The amphorae set up at street corners for use as urinals were in the open, and the purpose-built public toilets found in cities were multi-seaters without any sub-division. People were no doubt used to seeing people defecating wherever there was a convenient spot by the roadside, so there was less need for privacy in latrines. Even in private houses, the toilets were shielded from view by shoulder-high walls or wooden screens but do not appear to have had doors (Jansen 1997, 126, figs 10.5, 10.8).

A study of 195 toilets found in private houses at Pompeii show that most were situated in the working areas of the house, mainly in the kitchen or very near it, or alternatively in a courtyard or garden. Less commonly, they are found near the entrance to the house, while others are situated to take account of drains shared with other floors or neighbouring properties (Jansen 1997, 128). An investigation into room use of 30 *atrium* houses in the same town revealed that at least 16 out of 33 kitchens contained latrines, and 6 of the 11 examples of latrines in separate rooms were situated next to the kitchen (Allison 2004, table 5.14a, 103). The location in or near the kitchen was to help with the disposal of liquid wastes, which also helped to dilute or flush the toilets.

There were two main types of toilets at Pompeii: the flush toilet and the niche toilet. The flush toilet was chosen for the ground floors of houses well supplied with water, and had a tiled floor that was slightly higher than the surrounding area, sloping down to a drain at the back or side (Hobson 2009, figs 61, 122). There was a wooden seat over this floor, and often another wooden board to put the feet on when sitting down (Jansen 1997, 127). The toilet was flushed by water from a bucket or pot being poured over the sloping floor, not by piped water. Some kitchens had brick-built water storage tanks in them (filled by hand using buckets or, more rarely, supplied with piped water), which could be used to flush the toilet (*ibid.*, 130). Water might also need to be kept in or near the latrine for anal cleaning (if this method was used) or for the washing of hands (it may not have been a universal practice but the fictional Trimalchio certainly washed his hands after using a chamber pot, and offered water along with other facilities for any of his guests wanting to go to the toilet: Petronius, *Satyricon*, 27, 47).

The niche toilet was used in houses without a good water supply, or on the upper floors of buildings. It consisted of a niche built into the wall, so the person using it could not sit upright, but had to lean forward (see fig. 31). The toilet seat was placed directly over a drain pipe built into the wall, usually a series of interconnecting pottery pipes, so there was less need for water (Jansen 1997, 127, 130). At least some of the Pompeian toilets drained into cesspits, while others led to sewers. Elsewhere in the empire it is likely simpler versions of the pit latrine were used, when the seat was directly over the pit, without need of drains.

Latrines with cesspits can be satisfactory if the pit itself is kept dark enough so that it is unattractive to flies, if the latrine can be closed by a tight-fitting lid to keep the smell in and flies out, if the floor can be easily washed and if the pit is lined towards the top to avoid collapse. Examples are known that have been in use for over 20 years without any nuisance from smell or flies (Pickford 1995, 39, 43). Unfortunately, it is rare that all these requirements can be fulfilled. Modern reasons for disliking pit latrines focus mainly on the smell, but other reasons include the presence of flies, mosquitoes in wet pits, the danger of children falling into them through the toilet seats, the danger of adults falling in due to the collapse of either the timber seating or the walls of the pits, and the mess involved when emptying the pit. There is also the danger of the contents polluting surrounding ground water (Pickford 1995, 33, 39, 45; Khanna and Khanna 2006, 30).

The rate of accumulation of solids in a pit has been estimated at anything from between 40 to 90 litres per person per year (Pickford 1995, 41). The frequency with which the pit would need to be cleaned out would depend on the size of the pit, the surrounding soil type, the number of people using it, the method used for anal cleaning and how much other waste material was thrown in it, although in some modern examples it was found that pits deeper than 4m never completely filled, with sewage percolating into the surrounding soil (Pickford 1995, 43). The pit could therefore need to be emptied every few months or every few years. The operation involved men using buckets or pots to scoop material out of the pit, either straight into a container, such as a barrel put in position nearby, or else carrying each bucket load out to a container on a wagon outside. Either way, the containers had to be carried through house or garden, inevitably creating a stink and leaving a trail of spilt sewage (cf. Jansen 2000b, figs 4–5). At Pompeii, the mouth of the cesspit was often in an adjoining garden (Jansen 1997, fig. 10.9), or, even better, in the street itself, to cut down the mess involved in emptying it, although at least one was situated in the kitchen itself (*ibid.*, 132).

Due to the unpleasantness involved in emptying pits, in modern times householders usually pay someone else to do it (Pickford 1995, 52). Although Roman householders could in theory get their slaves to empty the pits, they would still need containers to put the contents in, a vehicle to carry it away and access to somewhere to dump it, so it is likely that it was also common practice for Romans to pay for this service. A graffito from Herculaneum records that someone paid 11 *asses* to have a cesspit emptied (*CIL*

4, no 10606; this was not hugely expensive, when compared with a graffito in Pompeii that records a tavern selling a cup of wine for one *as*, better wine for two *asses* and the best wine for four *asses*: Cooley and Cooley 2004, H12).

After being removed from the pit, the contents still had to be disposed of. Those doing the disposing may not have been too concerned about where they got rid of it; three inscriptions from Rome dated *c*.89 BC mark the boundaries of an area where it was forbidden to cremate bodies or dump manure or animal carcasses (*CIL* 1.839). In modern times human waste tends to be dumped on any available open ground, thrown into rivers or the sea, put into another pit or trench, used untreated on agricultural land as a fertiliser or mixed with vegetable waste to make compost before being used as a fertiliser (Pickford 1995, 99), and its disposal was probably equally varied in the Roman period.

Toilet Paper and Equivalents

Modern parallels reveal a wide range of materials used for anal cleaning, using both soft and hard materials: water, scrap paper, rags, leaves, grass, sticks, corncobs and stones, or combinations of these, have all been used (Pickford 1995, 32, 40). Excavations have indicated that moss and small squares of cloth were used in the medieval period, and similar cloths, wads of fine felted flax or other fibres, and bundles of coarser fibres were used in the post-medieval period (Carver 1979, 75; Robinson 1987, 21–3).

It is likely that the Romans used a variety of different methods, according to local traditions and what material was available to them. While rural communities would have used plants that could easily be collected locally, city dwellers may have had more difficulty finding suitable material. A fig tree planted near a toilet in a house in Pompeii has been suggested as a possible source of large leaves (Jansen 1997, 123, n. 8). Sherds of pottery found in a cesspit may simply have been general rubbish thrown in, as animal bones were also found (*ibid.*, 132), but they could possibly have been used for anal cleaning. It has been suggested moss found in the material from the latrines at Bearsden may have been used for this purpose, as it is known to have been used in later periods (Hobson 2009, 140).

The most famous form of Roman 'toilet paper' is the sponge on a stick used in the Mediterranean region, which could be washed and reused (Seneca, *Letters*, 70.20; Martial, *Epigrams*, 12.48.8). A number of assumptions about this method are often confidently repeated (that everyone carried their own; that they were washed out in vinegar; that the water channels in multi-seater latrines were for washing them out), when it is unclear how common this method actually was, even in the heart of the empire. Catullus' reference to burning a copy of a literary work called the *Annals of Volusius* that he described as being fit only for use as toilet paper suggests other methods were also used there (*Poems*, 36.1, 18–20).

REMOVAL OF SEWAGE

Use of Solid Waste

Compost made from human faeces is a valuable commodity today in some parts of the world, and has been equally well valued for many centuries and by many different cultures (Pickford 1995, 65–6; Hodge 1992, 336), and it is likely that those Romans who were paid to empty pits could make further money by selling the contents. It was certainly valued in the countryside, being seen as one of the best types of fertiliser available (Columella, *On Farming*, 1.6.24, 10.86, 11.3.12; Varro, *On Farming*, 1.38.2). Varro describes the design of a two-part manure pit, with one half for the fresh manure and the other for the manure ready for use, and mentions that sometimes farmers situated a portable toilet for the household over the pit to collect the raw material (*ibid.*, 1.13.4). Columella recommends that a farmer should always have fertiliser at hand, even if no manure is available; he advises collecting greenery from the roadside and from neighbours and mixing them with:

> the cleanings from his enclosure; he may sink a trench … and may heap together in one pile his ashes, sewer filth, straw and other dirt that is swept out … They can gather and heap together not only the waste matter from their own bodies, but also the dirt which the yard and the buildings produce every day. (*On Farming*, 2.14.6–8)

Use of Liquid Waste

Diluted urine could also be used as a fertiliser, but had many other uses because of its ammonia content. Households that produced their own cloth may have kept urine in barrels or reused amphorae for fulling new cloth or cleaning used clothes. Professional fullers, who needed large quantities of urine, put pots out in the street for passers-by to fill. These pots could be left there for some time, either to let the ammonia concentrate, or simply because the fuller could not be bothered to empty them when they were full. Martial unkindly comments that a woman called Thais 'smells worse than the old pot of a stingy fuller, recently broken in the middle of the road' (*Epigrams*, 6.93, see also 12.48). Since urine could be used by large businesses such as tanning and fulling as well as in agriculture, the Emperor Vespasian levied a tax on the urine collected from public toilets. A well-known story has him holding up a gold coin and asking if it smelt of urine when his son complained about this method of making money (Suetonius, *Vespasian*, 23).

11

DISPOSAL: RUBBISH

As there was no centralised system in the modern sense for the removal of rubbish to large dumps out of sight and smell of areas of habitation, in Roman times there would have been much more rubbish lying round in public places, and probably also within houses. However, the quantity and composition of household rubbish to be disposed of would have been different to that of the modern world. A study of waste disposal in Asia shows that while rich-income countries produce up to *c.*5.1kg of waste per capita per day, poor-income countries only produce up to *c.*0.9kg (Hoornweg and Thomas 1999, 7).

Table 5: Composition of Waste in Modern High- and Low-income Countries, Shown as a Percentage (after Hoornweg and Thomas 1999, table 2)

	High-income countries	Low-income countries
Paper and plastic	45	9
Organic	28	41
Metal and glass	15	3
Other	12	47

In high-income countries much of the waste consists of paper and plastic (mainly packaging, especially of food, but also newspapers and magazines), followed by organic waste from food. In low-income countries the largest proportion of the waste comes under the category of 'other', which includes ceramics, textiles and bone, but is usually mainly ash from wood fires (the use of coal produces an even higher percentage of ash), followed by an almost equally high percentage of organic waste (*ibid.*, 8, 13, 33).

COMPOSITION OF WASTE

Since organic material does not usually survive on Roman sites, it is difficult to gauge the relative quantities of waste that were discarded at this period. Some items would have had a secondary use before being fully discarded, such as clothing used as cleaning rags, while other waste became raw material for new objects, such as animal bone used to make counters, and yet other material had enough monetary value to prompt recycling.

Ash from the Fire

In some developing countries ash from the fire is used to soak up the grease on pans and dishes before they are rinsed in water, and it is possible that ashes were used for this purpose during the Roman period. Ash could also be used to make lye, a mild detergent for washing clothes and pots that was also used as a medicine, although the bulk of the ashes would still remain for disposal. Wood ash contains potash, phosphorus and potassium, and therefore makes a good fertiliser, especially as a light dressing before sowing (White 1970, 142). Columella refers to 'the use of ashes and cinders' as being beneficial, and Pliny mentions farmers who prefer it to dung (*On Farming*, 2.14.5; *Natural Histories*, 17.5.49). Ashes could also be added to the compost heap. Columella's recipe for a fertiliser included a mixture of brambles, sweepings, sewage and ashes (*ibid.*).

Food Remains

Animal Bones

Animal bone was sometimes used to make household items such as counters, dice, spindle whorls, weaving tablets, spoons and scapula scoops, as well as being used professionally by couch makers (MacGregor 1985, 181, 187, 191, 197, fig. 96). This would have used up only a very small proportion of the animal bone refuse produced. While some animal bones would have been eaten by dogs and other animals, most were simply thrown out, and broken animal bones are common on Roman sites where the soil condition allows survival. A study of ditch fills at the fort of Ribchester revealed that less than 10 per cent of cattle bones showed signs of being chewed by dogs but 30–40 per cent of sheep or pig fragments did. This raises the possibility that the large cattle bones were removed before the meat was cooked, and the bones were quickly buried as butchery waste, while the sheep and pigs may have been cooked with the meat still on the bones which were then dumped at a later stage as food remains, having been left lying round long enough for dogs to have access to them (Stallibrass 2000, 159).

Vegetable Matter

In later periods, food scraps and unwanted vegetable parts were often fed to a pig to be converted into meat. Plautus refers to millers feeding waste to pigs (*The Captives*, 807–10), and domestic households may also have done the same in those parts of the empire where pork and other pig products were commonly eaten (such as in Italy itself), but this does not seem to have been universal. In Britain pig products do not seem to have been so common, but were rather a special food, most often eaten in urban sites (Cool 2006, 82–4).

Pottery Vessels

The various mentions of potsherds in texts which suggest that they were a frequent sight are easily confirmed by excavations on Roman sites where pieces of pots are amongst the most common finds. In the novel by Petronius characters returning in the darkness after a meal dragged their 'bleeding feet nearly a whole hour over the flints and broken pots which lay out in the road' (*Satyricon*, 79). Columella says that young bees escaping from a beehive should be frightened by rattling bronze items or by 'potsherds, which are usually to be found lying about' (*On Farming*, 9.12.2), while a potsherd could be used to carry embers or prop up a wobbly table (Petronius, *Satyricon*, 136; Ovid, *Metamorphoses*, 8.662). Throwing sherds at crows was the equivalent of a modern 'wild goose hunt' (Persius, *Satires*, 3.60; Morton Braund 2004, 80, n. 16).

Modern studies of the use-life of non-glazed pots show their survival rates depend on what their function was and their size, with vessels used on ground-level hearths being more at risk than those used on higher stoves, as were those in households with children and small animals (Shott 1996, 464). Those with 'passive' use, such as water storage, lasted longer than those with 'active' use, such as cooking over a fire. The use-life can vary considerably between cultures, but in some cooking pots can have a use-life as low as a year or two, while those used for storage nearer 10 years (*ibid.*, table 2).

Some pottery sherds were reused. Peña lists 26 reuses for amphorae, but other pottery types were typically used for discs of varying sizes, the small ones probably as gaming counters and the larger ones as counting tallies and possibly as lids for small containers. Some pierced with a central hole are often identified as spindle whorls, but they may also be counting tallies since they are found in such large numbers. Examples, pierced and unpierced, are found on most Roman sites, ranging from roughly finished discs to those with the edges carefully filed down.

In some provinces, pieces of broken pottery were also used for writing. At Oxyrhynchus in Egypt such sherds (called *ostraca*) were often used to write delivery notes or receipts, with examples recording how much corn was loaded on to boats, accounts mentioning 7000 pickled fish (at 56 *drachmae* per 100) and 350 cakes (5 *drachmae* per 100), and receipts for 250 jars of wine (Grenfell and Hunt 2007, 358, 363–4, 366–7). The sherds could be left untrimmed and irregular, or else trimmed to a more regular shape (Peña 2007, fig. 6.13).

A dropped pot breaks into large and small fragments, but the large pieces are not found in the archaeological record unless they were thrown away in a place that was not disturbed at a later period, such as packing in postholes or drains that were never subsequently cleaned out. Sherds from the same vessel often end up widely scattered, suggesting the broken pieces have had an active life, being moved between temporary dumps and rubbish tips or fields.

Old Clothes

Due to the expense of cloth, clothes would be patched and reused as much as possible by the poor, and be cut up to use as patchwork for slaves (Columella, *On Farming*, 1.8.9). Clothes could also be torn into rags used for cleaning and polishing, for use as menstrual cloths and as toilet paper. Excavations at Vindolanda from 1973 to 1988 produced over 600 fragments of cloth, few of them larger than 20 x 20cm, and most much smaller. They included a fragment of a cloak remodelled for an unknown secondary use, a sock, an insole cut from what was probably originally a cloak, bandages or strapping, fragments of tunics or soft furnishings, and mending patches (Wild 1993, 84–5).

Paper and Papyrus

Pieces cut from old books and scrolls could be reused as wrapping paper before being thrown away. They were used for wrapping merchandise as varied as olives, pepper, fish, incense and perfume (Statius, *Silvae,* 4.9.10–4, Horace, *Histories*, 2.2.268–70; Catullus, *Poems*, 95.9; cf. Pliny, *Natural Histories*, 12.26.45, 13.23.76), and could be used to wrap fish before cooking (Statius, *Silvae*, 4.9.10–4). They could also be used as toilet paper.

Glass

Glass sherds were sometimes reused, especially for making discs, but also as sharp-edged blades. Usually, however, broken glass was collected for re-melting (Price and Cottam 1998, 7, 9). In the city of Rome it is known that broken glass was not just collected, but exchanged for low-value goods by street hawkers for later resale (Martial, *Epigrams*, 1.4.3–5; Juvenal, *Satires*, 5.48; Keller 2005, 67–8). Large quantities of glass have been found stored in pits at glass-making sites which must have been collected for recycling (Price and Cottam 1998, 5, 8; Keller 2005, 66). It seems to have been generally considered a cheap commodity traded only locally, although a barrel of cullet (crushed glass) found as part of a cargo of a Roman ship trading in wine and olive oil suggests longer-distance trading was sometimes worthwhile (*ibid.*, 68).

Copper Alloy

Broken copper-alloy fittings were collected and could be either sold to bronze workers, or else supplied to them as a raw material or given in part-exchange for replacement pieces. Examples can be found on many sites, such as a partially melted harness fitting and bead fused together from Wallsend Roman fort. Pliny refers to scrap metal, 'that is, copper or bronze that has been bought up after use', being added to the blend when making statues and tablets (*Natural Histories*, 34.20.97). Statues themselves could be reused, melted down to make 'little jugs, basins, frying-pans and chamber-pots' (Juvenal, *Satires*, 10.64; cf. Martial, *Epigrams*, 11.11.5–6).

METHOD OF DISPOSALS

Two studies of modern rubbish disposal in rural settlements in Guatemala and Syria show that there can be a range of strategies for getting rid of different materials (Peña 2007, 274–5). Ashes and house-sweepings are dumped in out-of-the-way places within the house compound, scattered over garden plots, or just thrown over a compound wall. Food waste is fed to animals and combustible rubbish is burnt as fuel. Other household refuse, such as broken or unwanted items, is often disposed of in two stages, first being kept in storerooms, in unused parts of the house, along the exterior walls of buildings, against the walls in corners of compounds or courtyards, or in abandoned buildings. At a later stage, when enough has accumulated, the material is collected together and taken further away from the compound or house. This final disposal site is rarely more than a two-minute walk away and could consist of pits, individual or communal middens usually situated near the edge of the settlement, or in a natural feature such as a ravine. Settlements situated near streams or rivers usually just throw the rubbish in the water.

Another study, of rubbish disposal in Southern India, showed that household refuse is thrown out on to a heap in an open area not too far away from the house, where the organic material would decompose, and then at intervals this material would be removed and spread over the fields (Khanna and Khanna 2006, 33). In the villages the rubbish (crop residue, kitchen waste and human excreta) is piled up in an open yard a few metres away from the house and left to compost. Although convenient for throwing rubbish out without having to go too far, the drawbacks are that it can drain unchecked in any direction, including back towards the house, and it attracts large numbers of insects (Chowde Gowda 1995, 157–8). Up to 77 per cent of the waste produced is reused as fuel for cooking, as animal fodder or as organic fertiliser. The effect is that 'the mixed odour of decaying human excreta and the smoke from the efficient burning of biomass fuels heralds one's approach to the villages' (*ibid.*, 159).

Collection within the House

Due to their mixed methods of disposal, the different types of rubbish were unlikely to have been collected in one place in a bin, as in a modern western household, but containers may have been used for certain categories, such as the ash from cooking fires which must have been collected from the hearth in some form of bucket or cask. Baskets often seem to have been useful containers; in the tale of the town and country mice, food left over from a previous meal was kept in baskets (Horace, *Satires*, 2.6.105), while glass collected for recycling was found in a basket in a cellar of the villa at Pisonella, near Boscoreale, Italy (Keller 2005, 66), and unwanted papyri were found in baskets on the rubbish tips of Oxyrhynchus (Grenfell and Hunt 2007, 349), although in this case the baskets themselves had also been thrown away.

Rubbish Dumps

The most common method of getting rid of rubbish was simply to pile it up in one location, where the organic components could rot down. These could be individual household mounds or massive city dumps (cf. Parsons 2007, pl. 7). The mounds would have smelt noticeably, as most would also include human faeces, since there was no division between sewage and other waste in the Roman period, as well as rotting food remains, including animal bones with the remains of flesh on them (as found in the rubbish tips at Mons Claudianus in Egypt: Peña 2007, 287).

Pits and Natural Features

In some cases pits were dug which could then be filled with refuse. To avoid the work involved in digging a pit, wherever possible any existing pit that was available was filled instead, such as disused wells (cf. Khanna and Khanna 2006, 33). Excavations within Roman towns have revealed undisturbed deposits of rubbish in 'the substructures of buildings, cisterns, pits, natural declivities, and cul-de-sacs' (Peña 2007, 283). Material has also been found in narrow alleys between buildings and in ditches. Sometimes the ditches were no longer in use, and were being used as just another pit or natural feature, but a study of the animal bones from ditches at Ribchester Roman fort has shown that while the majority came from a ditch that was deliberately in-filled, ditches still in active use (as evidenced by a number of re-cuttings) were also used for a certain amount of rubbish disposal (Stallibrass 2000, 159). In this case it was apparently acceptable to have rotting animal carcasses abandoned unburied close to the settlement, as the bones included a pair of hind legs and 'an almost complete torso which had been heavily scavenged by dogs' (*ibid.*, 162).

Latrines

As the Romans made little distinction between rubbish and sewage, some rubbish would simply have been thrown into cesspits. At a site at Botromagno in southern Italy, the excavation of an agricultural villa dated between the mid-second century and *c.*70 BC revealed a pit in the corner of a room near the entrance that was identified as a latrine, with soil high in phosphates. It contained large quantities of animal bone, tile and pottery, much of which was relatively complete, as well as wood and a range of small household objects (Peña 2007, 308). Other cesspits in Pompeii, Cosa and Gorhambury also contain pottery and animal bone (*ibid.*, 309).

Bonfires

Bonfires were used on farms to get rid of sticks and other unwanted wood (Cato, *On Farming*, 38). At Vindolanda Roman fort, the remains of bonfires used to burn rubbish, including writing tablets, were found in the yard of the commanding officer's house and on the road between the house and the fort rampart (Birley 2002, 68). Unwanted wood could also be burnt as fuel. Material from an oven in the fort at Elginhaugh included alder, birch, hazel and oak wood, as well as a fragment of fir. As fir was not a native wood, this is likely to have been a container or something similar that was broken up and used for fuel when no longer needed (Clapham 2007, 586–7).

Dogs and Pigs

Some of the organic rubbish would be scavenged by dogs, either strays or household-owned ones which were not fully fed within the house. Such dogs would not be fussy eaters and would eat anything available. A study of free-ranging domestic dogs in rural Zimbabwe (where leftover food was thrown into pits at the perimeter of house yards) showed that the dogs' diet was made up of 24 per cent cereal/vegetable matter, 50 per cent meat/carrion, 22 per cent faeces and 4 per cent other matter (Butler and du Toit 2002, 30, table 2). In this study, 88 per cent of the dogs' diet was derived from humans, largely due to the disposal of food waste in easily accessible pits close to the house and the fact that human faeces were freely available due to open defecation (*ibid.*, 34). Martial mentions dogs eating human faeces when considering the final fate of a meal: 'a matter for a luckless sponge on a doomed stick or some dog or other, or a pot by the roadside to take care of' (*Epigrams*, 12.48.7–8; *cf.* 1.83).

Pigs are equally unfussy eaters, and as well as being deliberately given waste food, they may also have scavenged amongst discarded rubbish, both in rural settlements and cities. In historic times, pigs foraged in the streets of New York as late as the nineteenth century, and in Naples tethered pigs were used to clear up the area in front of the their owners' houses, as the city had no organised street cleaning, while in Cairo rubbish collectors still raise pigs in the streets (Miller 1990, 125, n. 2, 126). In the Roman period it was common for bakers to keep pigs that were fed on waste (such as the waste bran from milling); a character in Plautus' play *The Captives* complains about seeing these pigs in public places, where they may well have been foraging (Columella, *On Farming*, 7.9.2; Plautus, *The Captives*, 806–10).

RURAL SETTLEMENTS

Ash could be scattered over vegetable plots or fields, or added to midden heaps along with the other household rubbish; Arrian also refers to a small vessel or implement being thrown out onto a manure pile (Peña 2007, 309). The material from the midden

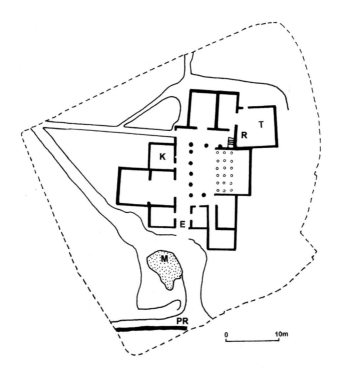

Fig. 32 Rubbish disposal at Villa Regina, near Pompeii. E = main entrance; K = kitchen; M = midden heap; PR = public road; R = rubbish pile; T = threshing floor. (After Peña 2007)

heaps would eventually be spread over the fields as fertiliser. The excavation of the Villa Regina, a country house near Pompeii, shows a variety of disposal methods which probably reflects the different stages involved in rubbish disposal. The house was being repaired at the time of the eruption and may not have been occupied (see fig. 32), since the kitchen was certainly not in use, as the floor (including the raised hearth) was covered with a 0.5m layer of ash. There was a dump of rubbish (mainly building material) in the corner of the open drying/threshing floor, and a further concentration along the enclosure road that bordered the public road, while the surrounding vineyards had a thin scatter of artefacts suggesting the spreading of midden material as fertiliser. Outside the main entrance of the villa, to be skirted by any visitor approaching the building, was a midden heap consisting of burnt material and broken objects, while there may have been further heaps outside the area of excavation (ibid., 310–6).

MILITARY ESTABLISHMENTS

There is evidence that at least in the first century the army made an effort to keep military establishments clean. The legionary fortress at Usk produced so little glass it is assumed there was an organised system of collecting it for recycling (Keller 2005, 66). Rubbish was probably collected in an organised manner and taken outside the walls to midden heaps, as at Vindonissa in Switzerland. The legionary fortress was set on a plateau between two rivers, sloping down steeply on the north side to the River Aare. This slope was used as a rubbish dump between c.47 and 101. The original size of the dump is unknown, but by the time it was excavated it was 50m long by 14m wide and 13m high; it produced approximately 200,000 objects (Ettlinger 1951, 105; Macdonald 1935, 249). It consisted of two parts, material dumped up to c.70 and material dumped from 70–101, divided by a layer of demolition material. The later portion of the dump had successive layers of heavy timbers that were taken to be the remains of timber roadways laid out for the carts bringing the waste out from the fort (ibid.).

The fortress at York was also kept fairly clean until the fourth century, with organised dumping of rubbish outside its walls. In a building of unknown use within the fortress on the Blake Street site, the higher-status range of rooms was kept clean, with pottery sherds only found in open areas such as the courtyard. A lower-status range within the building was not kept as clean, so that while the centre of the rooms were clear, pottery sherds (and no doubt other rubbish) accumulated round the edges (ibid., 1993). By the fourth century, material seems to have been dumped over internal roads and finally even within buildings, probably because parts of the fortress were no longer being fully used (Monaghan 1993, 743). A comparison of the quantities of organic material found at the Blake Street site (barrack blocks inside the fortress) and at the general accident site (a service area sometimes used as a dumping ground outside the fortress) also suggests that the military kept the fortress clean (Hall *et al.* 1990, 389).

The desire not to have to walk too far to get rid of rubbish can also been seen at Mons Claudianus in Egypt, a fort and quarry settlement with a population of no more than 920 inhabitants (Peña 2007, 284–9). The fort was kept free of waste for about 30 years, with the refuse thrown out on to two middens within the civilian settlement. One, in use for about 40 years, was approximately 70m long and 18m wide, and the second was about 110m long and 15m wide. From the early 140s, however, rubbish began to be dumped on the roads and in unoccupied buildings inside the fort. In room 1 of the building Fort North 1, for example, the rubbish reached to the top of the walls, so while the early material could have been thrown in through the door, the later material must have been thrown in from an upper room, or (if the building was roofless) tossed over the walls. Rooms with surviving roofs also had rubbish piled on top of them.

TOWNS AND CITIES

People living in towns and cities, especially the poor, had little opportunity to dispose of cooking ash on vegetable plots and even less opportunity to use their rubbish as fertiliser for fields. The quantities of waste produced and the lack of opportunities for the producers to reuse any of it or possess space to dispose of it suggests that in the larger towns and cities, and especially in Rome, there was some system for the collection of rubbish. Those people living on the upper storeys of large tenement buildings often could not be bothered to take their rubbish down to street level, let alone any further away, and simply threw waste out of their windows. Roman law said that people should be able to walk public streets without fear of injury, and jurists discussed who would be liable if passers-by were injured by objects falling on them in the street. Chapter 3 in Book 9 of the *Digest of Justinian* was entitled 'those who pour or throw things out of buildings', and started with the statement: 'If anything should be thrown out or poured out from a building onto a place where people commonly pass and re-pass or stand about, I will grant an action to be brought against whoever lives there for double the damage caused or done as a result.' However, unless the person was caught in the act, trying to work out exactly who had thrown what from which window in close-set buildings would have proved difficult. The stuff being thrown out could include food waste, waste water and sewage, but also more dangerous objects. Juvenal refers to the tall buildings and 'how often cracked and broken pots fall from windows, with what force they mark and damage the road metalling when they strike it' (*Satires*, 3.268–71).

In law, individuals were responsible for cleaning their own part of the road:

> each person is to keep the public street outside his own house in repair and clean out the open gutters and ensure that no vehicle is prevented from access. Occupiers of rented accommodation must carry out these repairs themselves if the owner fails to do so and deduct their expenses from the rent. [The city officials] must see to it that nothing is left outside workshops, except for a fuller leaving out clothing to dry, or a carpenter putting out wheels; and these are not by doing so to prevent a vehicle from passing. They are not to allow anyone to fight in the streets, or to fling dung, or to throw out any dead animals or skins. (*Digest*, 43.10.1)

A law of 44 BC relating to the city of Rome stipulated that house owners had to keep their part of the road in order, and that if they did not, city officials would get a contractor to do it and then charge the house owner. The officials were responsible for the 'public' roads:

> nothing in this law is intended to prevent the incumbent aediles (the *quattuorviri* for cleaning the streets within the city, the *duoviri* for cleaning the roads outside but within one mile of the city of Rome) from seeing to the cleaning of the public roads, and having full power in such matters. (Tablet of Heraclea: Lewis and Reinhold 1966, section 161)

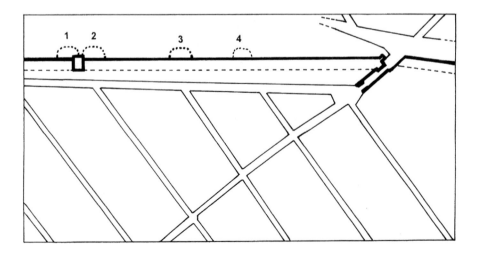

Fig. 33 The north wall of Pompeii near the Porta di Nola showing the location of rubbish dumps. (After Peña 2007)

0   50m

The evidence for smaller towns is not so clear, but a study of two rich houses in Pompeii, one near the centre and one by the city wall, has shown that there must have been some system for the removal of waste, since larger animal bones were consistently absent from the food waste. Neither house had rubbish pits within its precinct, and while those living in one of the houses, near the city wall, could have simply thrown their waste over the wall, to join other refuse already dumped there, the other house in the centre of the town must have got rid of its rubbish in some other way, possibly by household members transporting it to one of the city dumps (Ciaraldi and Richardson 2000, 79, 81). A deposit outside the Porta Ercolana, said to be a rubbish dump, was 250m long and up to 1.5m deep (Peña 2007, 279). An excavation of a length of wall from the Porta di Nola has revealed two midden heaps against the town wall either side of Tower 8, and two more that roughly line up with the ends of the roads leading up to the wall, suggesting public disposal (see fig. 33).

Three of the four heaps were excavated, and had the following dimensions:

	L	W	D (m)
1.	6	3	0.85
2.	5	3	0.58
3.	13	3	0.85

The excavation report refers to pottery, building material, lamps and artefacts of bronze, glass and bone; it can be assumed the mounds also included animal bone, although this is not mentioned (*ibid.*, 279–82).

At Oxyrhynchus in Egypt a large number of the town rubbish mounds survived until the end of the last century, the tallest of which were between 7.6–10.6m high when excavated. Some of the mounds stood alone while some spread out to join with others, forming ridges of refuse. Many were surprisingly close to important civic works such as the theatre and the colonnaded main road (see fig. 34). As the town contracted in size over the succeeding centuries, the rubbish tips moved in closer to the surviving core of the settlement, although some of the original ones seem to have been in use for several hundred years (Grenfell and Hunt 2007, 349). The excavators found that one set was 'a long, narrow range of mounds of which the eastern part had accumulated in the second and third centuries, while the western part was mainly composed of fourth or fifth century rubbish with earlier layers underneath' (*ibid.*, 360). Nothing is known about who started the separate mounds, who could use them or why new ones were started (*ibid.*, 348, 353–5, 360, 362, 365).

Some of the mounds were made up, as is perhaps to be expected, of mixed material, often laid down in clearly defined dump lines. The excavators recorded that 'the particular mixture of earth mixed with straw and bits of wood in which papyrus is found ... sometimes runs in clearly marked strata between other layers

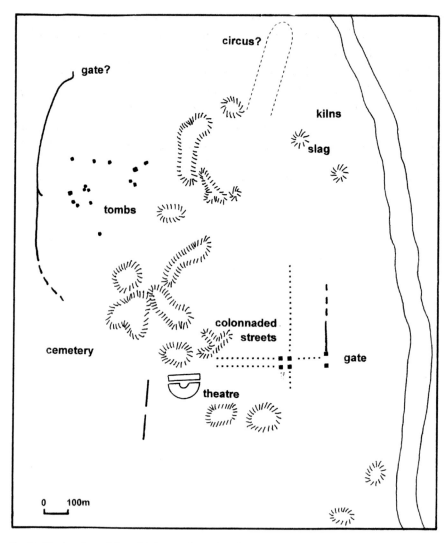

Fig. 34 The location of the rubbish tips of Oxyrhynchus, Egypt in relation to the known features of the town. (Information taken from Bowman *et al.* 2007)

of cinders, bricks or all kinds of debris' (Turner 2007, 21). Other mounds 'consisted entirely of ashes' or 'mainly of cinders', suggesting there was some form of control over who could use the mound or what could be dumped there (Grenfell and Hunt 2007, 350, 353). The mounds seem to have contained a wide range of material, with the excavators recording, amongst other objects, broken amphorae, glass, coins, lead tokens, dice, hair pins, tools, reed pens, lamps, brushes, combs, wooden implements, clay moulds, rag dolls, baskets, socks, shoes and even some loaves of bread (*ibid.*, 351, 355, 359). One of their discoveries was a large quantity of papyrus that had been thrown out from a local archive: the 'old papyrus rolls were put in baskets or on wicker trays and thrown away as rubbish ... it was the practice to tear most of the rolls to pieces first' (*ibid.*, 349).

In St Albans in England, the contraction of the town in the fourth century also resulted in rubbish being deposited close to the town centre rather than at the edges of the settlement. As with the military examples already mentioned, this is another example where an empty, abandoned building was used as a convenient dumping ground. In this case, the central area of the theatre, situated less than 100m from the Forum, was found to be filled with 1.5m-thick layer of household rubbish (Kenyon 1935, 239–40).

12

CONCLUSIONS

The time spent on housework in the Roman world could be considerable, but in contrast to modern housework, less time was spent on cleaning floors or dusting furniture and more time on the supply of basics such as water and fuel. These two necessities required a considerable input of time and effort (and often money as well for those living in cities). Wherever possible such work was carried out by slave labour. In the richer households the large number of slaves could allow for specialisations, such as the male slaves who were full-time water carriers, but in most households slaves had to carry out a wide range of jobs. Only one of the many tasks that made up Roman housework was considered to be 'women's work', and that was spinning; all other tasks seem to have been carried out by both sexes.

Many aspects of Roman housework have parallels in the methods used throughout the succeeding centuries, in many cases up until the nineteenth century and sometimes even beyond. Washing clothes in rivers, for example, was still being recorded in travel books on Ireland and Scotland in the nineteenth century and into the early twentieth century (Davidson 1986, 141, fig. 86), while the collection of urine for use in fulling mills lasted until the early twentieth century in the area round Huddersfield (Hobson 2009, 139). In many cases, the methods are still in use to the current day. Washing clothes in rivers and drying them on the ground or spread over convenient bushes or fences is common in many countries, as is cooking over wood-fuelled fires (see plates 18, 19). Public water sources for collecting water, pit latrines, hand-emptied cesspits and open drains for getting rid of water are all still in widespread use (see plate 20). According to the WHO/UNICEF *Joint Monitoring Programme for Drinking-water Supply and Sanitation* of 2008 open defecation is practised by 778 million people in Southern Asia alone, and globally by 18 per cent of the entire world's population. Housework is one of the few areas of Roman life where the methods employed would be instantly recognisable to a vast number of people alive today, whether it is fetching water from a well, grinding grain in a quern, beating clothes clean in running water or tossing rubbish out on to a midden heap.

APPENDIX

ANCIENT AUTHORS

Unless otherwise stated in the text, all the quotations from ancient authors are taken from the translations of the Loeb Classical Library.

Ammianus Marcellinus, late fourth century AD
Histories

He was born to a noble family in the eastern part of the empire, probably Antioch, and served as a soldier. Only 18 volumes of his *Histories*, covering the period 353–78 survive. They include eyewitness accounts of some events by the author.

Anonymous, first century BC
Moretum

This poem was originally thought to have been by Virgil, but is more likely to have been by an anonymous contemporary. A *moretum* is a cheese and vegetable paste.

Apuleius, second century AD
Metamorphoses; A Discourse on Magic

He was born in Numidia, Africa, studied at Carthage and Athens and travelled widely before returning to settle in Carthage. *Metamorphoses* (also known as *The Golden Ass*) is a novel recounting the various adventures of a man called Lucius who was transformed into a donkey. *A Discourse on Magic* is an account of an accusation made against Apuleius that he used magic to win a rich wife and the defence he made against the charge.

Augustine, late fourth to early fifth century AD
Letters

He was born in Thagaste, Numidia. He became a professor of rhetoric at Milan and, after converting to Christianity, became Bishop of Hippo in Numidia.

Aulus Gellius, second century AD
Attic Nights

He was educated in Athens and lived in Rome. *Attic Nights* is a 20-volume compilation of random notes on grammar, philosophy and history and numerous other topics, culled from various works and from the conversations of friends, which he had first collected together during winter nights while he was living in Attica.

Caesar, first century AD
Civil War

A commentary on Caesar's role in the Civil War.

Cato, second century BC
On Farming

This book is one of the first surviving works written in Latin. It is a practical handbook written for fellow landowners living in southern Italy, and includes the names of the best places to buy various pieces of equipment.

Catullus, first century BC
Poems

He was born to a wealthy family in Verona in northern Italy and moved to Rome as a young man.

Cicero, first century BC
Letters; On the Nature of the Gods

He was born to a wealthy family in Arpinum, Italy. He was educated in Rome and had a successful career as a lawyer and politician, until he made an enemy of Mark Antony. Over 800 letters by Cicero to friends and family survive. *On the Nature of the Gods* is a philosophical discussion that includes descriptions of a large variety of different religions.

Claudian, c.AD 399
Epithalamium of Palladius and Celerina; Against Eutropius

He was a court poet to the Emperor Honorius. An *epithalamium* is a form of poem written for brides on their way to the marital chamber; this example was written by Claudian in honour of the marriage of his friend Palladius to Celerina.

Clement, late second or early third century AD
The Instructor

He was head of the Catechetical School of Alexandria. *The Instructor* is a three-volume book explaining how Christians should lead their everyday life, and is therefore disapproving of any type of luxurious living.

Columella, first century AD
On Farming

He was born in Gades in Spain, but spent much of his life in Italy, owning a number of different farms in central Italy. *On Farming* is a comprehensive treatise on Roman agricultural matters as carried out in the Mediterranean region, in 12 books.

Dio Cassius, late second or early third century AD
Roman History

He was born in Nicaea in Asia Minor, held various offices in Rome, and then retired to Nicaea before his death. He wrote an 89-volume history of Rome in Greek, although only the section covering the period 68 BC–AD 46 survives.

Dioscorides, first century AD
On Medical Matters

He was a Greek physician who practised in Rome. *On Medical Matters* is a five-volume encyclopaedia in Greek listing the plants, minerals and animals used in medicines.

Eusebius, late third to early fourth century AD
History of the Church

He was Bishop of Caesarea in Palestine. The *History*, written in Greek, records the rise of the church from the Apostles until his own time.

Frontinus, first century AD
On Aqueducts

Amongst his other official appointments, Frontinus was for a while governor of Britain. He was later commissioner of the water supply for Rome. *On Aqueducts* is a two-volume official report on the state of the aqueducts of Rome, based on his own research.

Fronto, second century AD
Correspondence

He was born in Cirta, Numidia and educated at Rome. He became a famous lawyer and orator, and was appointed by the Emperor to be tutor to Marcus Aurelius and Lucius Verus. Much of the *Correspondence* consists of letters to his pupils and their adoptive father Antoninus Pius, and their replies.

Horace, first century BC
Satires

He was born in Venusia, Italy, the son of a wealthy freedman, and educated in Rome and Athens. After all his property was confiscated he became a Treasury official for the rest of his life and found patrons for his poetry. The two volumes of the *Satires* advocate a simple life for happiness and contentment and mock worldly ambitions.

Isidore, early seventh century AD
Etymologies

He was born in Spain and later became Archbishop of Seville. He was also influential in the court of the Visigothic kings. The 20 volumes of the *Etymologies* are an encyclopaedia made up of brief entries on thousands of topics, including discussions of the origins of many of the terms used.

Juvenal, early second century AD
Satires

He lived at Rome and may have been of relatively high social status. The *Satires* are 16 poems in 5 volumes, consisting of indignant rants at the follies of Roman society.

Livy, late first century BC to early first century AD
History of Rome

He was born in Padua, Italy, and spent most of his life at Rome. He wrote a history of Rome from the foundation of the city to 9 BC, although only 35 volumes survive.

Lucian, second century AD
Poems

He was born in Samosata, Syria and travelled to Greece, Italy and Egypt. He was a teacher of rhetoric, writing in Greek.

Lucilius, second century BC
Satires

Born in southern Italy, he spent much of his life in Rome. Only fragments of his poetry have survived.

Lucretius, first century BC
On the Nature of Things

He was a wealthy man who probably owned a house in Rome as well as a country estate. *On the Nature of Things* is an unfinished poem in six volumes, explaining Epicurean philosophy.

Martial, late first century AD
Epigrams

He was born in Bilbilis in Spain, lived in Rome for many years, and returned to Spain a few years before his death. The *Epigrams* consist of 14 volumes of short witty poems and two-line mottoes to accompany gifts given at Saturnalia. The books were mainly written in Rome and reflect life in that city.

Ovid, late first century BC to early first century AD
Calendar; Metamorphoses; Remedies of Love

He was born in Sulmo near Rome and lived in Rome until he was banished to Tomis on the Black Sea. The *Calendar* is an unfinished poem in six volumes describing festivals and other seasonal information. *Metamorphoses* is a 15-volume collection of myths and stories involving shape-changers. *Remedies of Love* is a poem explaining how men can get women to fall out of love with them.

Persius, first century AD
Satires

He was a wealthy man who lived in Rome. A single book of six poems was published posthumously.

Petronius, first century AD
Satyricon

He lived in Rome and was part of the court of the Emperor Nero. The *Satyricon* is a comic novel recounting the adventures of Encolpius and his companions. Only fragments of the book now survive.

Plautus, second century BC
Stichus; *The Captives*; *The Comedy of Asses*; *The Merchant*; *The Persian*; *The Rope*; *The Two Menaechmuses*

He was born in central Italy and worked in Rome. He was a playwright who wrote a series of comedies, amongst the earliest surviving works written in Latin, of which parts of 20 survive. He reworked and adapted Greek originals in order to make them appeal to a Roman audience.

Pliny the Elder, first century AD
Natural Histories

He was born at Como, in northern Italy, and lived in Rome for a while, but travelled widely during his career. He held a long series of military, legal and administrative posts. The *Natural Histories* are a 37-volume encyclopaedia describing every aspect of plants, animals and minerals, and their uses, as well as geography, meteorology, horticulture, anthropology and much more. The information was compiled from a large number of earlier works without much discrimination or critical consideration.

Pliny the Younger, first and early second century AD
Letters

There are nine surviving books of his collected letters, as well as his official correspondence with Trajan when he was the emperor's special representative to the province of Bithynia–Pontus during the last years of his life.

Plutarch, late first and early second century AD
Moralia

He was born in Chaeronea in Greece, and spent much of his life there, although he travelled widely in his youth. The *Moralia* is a collection of 78 essays and speeches in Greek that cover a large number of mixed topics. Book 4 includes 'Roman and Greek questions', which describe the history or purpose of various customs of the Romans and Greeks.

Propertius, first century BC
Elegies

He worked in Rome, producing four volumes of poems.

Seneca, first century BC
Natural Questions; On Tranquillity of Mind

He was born in Corduba, Spain, and educated in Rome. *Natural Questions* are seven volumes on meteorology and other scientific matters, compiled from previous works. *On Tranquillity of Mind* is a philosophical dialogue.

SHA, Scriptores Historia Augusta, fourth century AD

A collection of 30 surviving biographies of the emperors from Hadrian to Carinus, written by a number of different authors. The style was copied from the biographies by Suetonius, and includes much on the personalities and private lives of the subjects. The biographies include numerous fictitious sources and trivial material to make the stories more interesting to their intended readership.

Soranus, second century AD
Gynecology

He was born in Ephesus and practised as a doctor at Alexandria and Rome. The four-volume *Gynecology* was written in Greek.

Statius, first century AD
Silvae

He was born in Naples and lived and worked in Rome. *Silvae* are five volumes of poems.

Suetonius, second century AD
Twelve Caesars

He practised law in Rome and held a number of posts in the imperial court. The series of 12 studies are collections of anecdotes and gossip on several themes rather than straightforward biographies.

Tacitus, late first and early second century AD
Annals

He was educated in Rome and became a lawyer and politician. The *Annals* are a 16-volume history of Rome from the death of Augustus to the death of Nero.

Valerius Maximus, first century AD
Memorable Sayings

He came from a poor family, but due to patronage became part of the same literary circle to which Ovid belonged. The book is a nine-volume compilation of historical stories with a strong moral tone, intended for use in schools of rhetoric.

Varro, first century BC
On the Latin Language; On Agriculture

He was born in Reate, in Italy. He had a villa at Casinum (*c*.130km south-east of Rome), studied in Athens and lived for a while in Rome. *On the Latin Language* was originally 25 volumes long, although only six books have survived, discussing the origins of Latin words (not always correctly). The three volumes of *On Agriculture* were intended as a practical handbook on agriculture and animal husbandry for his wife.

Vegetius, late fourth century AD
Epitome of Military Science

He was a horse breeder and bureaucrat who had travelled extensively. The book describes the organisation of the contemporary army and its activities and often compares it unfavourably to the army of the early empire, but Vegetius himself had no personal military experience and compiled the book from other works.

Venantius Fortunatus, sixth century AD
Poems

He was born in northern Italy, educated at Ravenna and later moved to Gaul, where he eventually became Bishop of Poitiers. There are 11 surviving books of miscellaneous poems.

Vitruvius, first century BC
On Architecture

He was a solider, engineer and architect, who produced a 10-volume work on architecture and engineering, drawing on both previous works and his own experience.

BIBLIOGRAPHY

Adam, J. 2005 *Roman Building: Materials and Techniques*, Abingdon

Anon. 1999 *Tanzania: Social Sector Review*, World Bank Country Study

Anon. 2006 www.mum.org/pastgerm.htm

Allason-Jones, L. 2005 *Women in Roman Britain*, York

Allison, P.M. 2004 *Pompeian Households: an Analysis of the Material Culture*, Los Angeles

Bailey, D.M. 1996 *A Catalogue of the Lamps in the British Museum, Volume IV: Lamps of Metal and Stone, and Lampstands*, London

Bairoch, P. 1991 *Cities and Economic Development from the Dawn of History to the Present*, Chicago

Barney, S.A., Lewis, W.J., Beach, J.A. and Berghof, O. 2006 *The Etymologies of Isidore of Seville*, Cambridge

Beagrie, N. 1989 'The Romano-British pewter industry', *Britannia* 20, 169–91

Bidwell, P. 1985 *The Roman Fort of Vindolanda*, London

———. 2007 *Roman Forts in Britain*, Stroud

Birley, A. 2002 *Garrison Life at Vindolanda: a Band of Brothers*, Stroud

Blair, I., Spain, R., Swift, D., Taylor, T. and Goodburn, D. 2006 'Wells and bucket-chains: unforeseen elements of water supply in early Roman London', *Britannia* 37, 1–52

Blake, J. 1999 *Vindolanda Research Reports Volume IV: the Small Finds. Fascicule III: the Tools*, Greenhead

Blyth, P.H. 1999 'The consumption and cost of fuel in hypocaust baths', DeLaine, J. and Johnston, D.E. (eds), *Roman Baths and Bathing*, Journal of Roman Archaeology Supplementary series 37, 87–98

Boon, G.C. 1957 *Roman Silchester: the Archaeology of a Romano-British Town*, London

Bowles, S. 1866 *Across the Continent: a Summer's Journey to the Rocky Mountains, the Mormons and the Pacific*, New York

Bowman, A.K. 1994 *Life and Letters on the Roman Frontier*, London

Bowman, A.K., Coles, R.A., Gonis, G., Obbink, D. and Parsons, P.J. (eds) 2007
Oxyrhynchus: a City and its Texts, London

Bowman, A.K. and Thomas, J.D. 1994 *The Vindolanda Writing Tablets* (Tabulae
Vindolandenses II), London

Bradley, K. 1994 *Slavery and Society at Rome*, Cambridge

Bradley, M. 2002 '"It all comes out in the wash": looking harder at the Roman
fullonica', *Journal of Roman Archaeology* 15, 21–44

Broughton, S. D. 2005 *Letters from Portugal, Spain and France 1812-1814*, Stroud

Butler, J.R.A. and du Toit, J.T. 2002 'Diet of free-ranging domestic dogs (*Canis
familiaris*) in rural Zimbabwe: implications for wild scavengers on the periphery
of wildlife reserves', *Animal Conservation* 5, 29–37

Caley, E.R. 1926a 'Leiden Papyrus X: an English translation with brief notes', *Journal
of Chemical Education* 3.10, 1149–66

Caley, E.R. 1926b 'The Stockholm Papyrus: an English translation with brief notes',
Journal of Chemical Education 4.8, 979–1002

Carr, K. 2000 'Women's work: spinning and weaving in the Greek home', Cardon, D.
and Feugère, M. (eds), *Archéologie des Textiles des Origines au Ve Siècle*, Montagnac

Carver, M.O.H. 1979 'Three Saxo-Norman tenements in Durham City', *Medieval
Archaeology* 23, 55–76

Chapman, S. 1972 *The Cotton Industry in the Industrial Revolution*, London

Chowde Gowda, M. 1995 'Rural waste management in a South Indian village – a
case study', *Bioresource Technology* 53, 157–64

Ciaraldi, M. and Richardson, J. 2000 'Food, ritual and rubbish in the making of
Pompeii', Fincham, G., Harrison, G., Ridgers Holland, R. and Revell, L. (eds),
TRAC 99, Proceedings of the Ninth Annual Theoretical Roman Archaeology Conference,
Oxford, 74–82

CIL = Corpus Signorum Imperii Romani

Clapham. A.J. 2007 'Plant remains', Hanson, W.S., *Elginhaugh: a Flavian Fort and its
Annexe, Volume 2*, London

Clark, G. 1994 *Women in Late Antiquity: Pagan and Christian Life-styles*, Oxford

Clarke, J.R. 2003 *Art in the Lives of Ordinary Romans*, Berkeley

Cockle, H. 1981 'Pottery manufacture in Egypt: a new papyrus', *Journal of Roman
Studies* 71, 87–97

Connor, C.L. 1998 *The Color of Ivory: Polychromy on Byzantine Ivories*, Princeton

Cool, H.E.M. 2006 *Eating and Drinking in Roman Britain*, Cambridge

Cooley, A.E. and Cooley, M.G. 2004 *Pompeii: a Sourcebook*, Abingdon

Cottica, D. 2007 'Spinning in the Roman World: from everyday craft to metaphor
of destiny', Gillis, C. and Nosch, M.B. (eds), *Ancient Textiles: Production, Craft and
Society. Proceedings of the First International Conference in Ancient Textiles*, Oxford,
220–8

Croom, A.T. 2000 *Roman Clothing and Fashion*, Stroud
———. 2001 'Experiments in Roman military cooking', *Arbeia Journal* 6–7, 37–47
———. 2007 *Roman Furniture*, Stroud
Crow, J. 2004 *Housesteads; A Fort and Garrison on Hadrian's Wall*, Stroud
Crummy, P. 1984 *Excavations at Lion Walk, Balkerne Lane, and Middleborough, Colchester, Essex*, Colchester Archaeological Report 3
D'ambra, E. 2007 *Roman Women*, New York
Davidson, C. 1986 *A Woman's Work is Never Done: a History of Housework in the British Isles 1650–1950*, London
Dearne, M.J. and Branigan, K. 1995 'The use of coal in Roman Britain', *Antiquaries Journal* 75, 71–106
Dell'Orto, L.F. and Varone, A. 1992 *Rediscovering Pompeii*, Rome
Donalson, M.D. 1999 *The Domestic Cat in Roman Civilisation*, New York
Dore, J.N. and Gillam, J.P. 1979 *The Roman Fort at South Shields: Excavations 1875–1975*, Newcastle upon Tyne
Dunkerley, J., Macauley, M., Naimuddin, M. and Agarwal, P.C. 1990 'Consumption of fuelwood and other household cooking fuels in Indian cities', *Energy Policy* 18.1, 92–9
Eckardt, H. 1999 'The Colchester "child's grave"', *Britannia* 30, 111–32
———. 2002 *Illuminating Roman Britain*, Montagnac
Elias, N. 1994 *The Civilizing Process: the History of Manners and State Formation and Civilization*, Oxford
Estyn Evans, E. 2000 *Irish Folk Ways*, Mineola
Ettlinger, E. 1951 'Legionary pottery from Vindonissa', *Journal of Roman Studies* 41, 105–11
Fagan, G.G. 2002 *Bathing in Public in the Roman World*, Ann Arbor
Fink, R.O. 1971 *Roman Military Records on Papyrus*, Cleveland
Finley, H. 2006 www.mum.org/pastgerm.htm
Filbee, M. 1980 *A Woman's Place*, London
Forbes, R.J. 1955 *Studies in Ancient Technology, Volume 3*, Leiden
Frere, S.S. and Tomlin, R.S.O. 1992 *The Roman Inscriptions of Britain Volume II, Fascicule 4*, Stroud
Galloway, J.A., Keene, D. and Murphy, M. 1996 'Fuelling the city: production and distribution of firewood and fuel in London's region, 1290–1400', *Economic History Review* 49, 447–72
George, J. 1995 *Venantius Fortunatus: Personal and Political Poems*, Liverpool
Granger-Taylor, H. 1987 'The Emperor's clothes: the fold lines', *Bulletin of the Cleveland Museum of Art* 74.3, 114–23
Graser, E.R. 1975 'The Edict of Diocletian', Frank, T. (ed.), *An Economic Survey of Ancient Rome, Volume 5: Rome and Italy of the Empire*, New York

Grenfell, B.P. and Hunt, A.S. 2007 'Excavations at Oxyrhynchus (1896–1907)' Bowman *et al.* 2007, 345–68

Guppy, S. 1989 *The Blindfold Horse: Memories of a Persian Childhood*, London

Haines, C.R. 1988 *The Correspondence of Marcus Cornelius Fronto*, Cambridge

Hall, A.R., Kenward, H.K. and O'Connor, T.P. 1990 'Discussion and synthesis', Hall, A.R. and Kenward, H.K., *Environmental Evidence from the* Colonia: *General Accident and Rougier Street*, Archaeology of York 14, fascicule 6

Handler, S. 2001 *Austere Luminosity of Chinese Classical Furniture*, Berkeley

Hobson, B. 2009 Latrinae et Foricae: *Toilets in the Roman World*, London

Hodge, A.T. 1992 *Roman Aqueducts and Water Supply*, London

Hoornweg, D. and Thomas, L. 1999 *What a Waste: Solid Waste Management in Asia*, World Bank Working Paper

Humphrey, J.W., Oleson, J.P. and Sherwood, A.N. 1998 *Greek and Roman Technology: a Sourcebook*, London

Jansen, G. 1997 'Private toilets at Pompeii; appearance and operation', Bon, S.E. and Jones, R. (eds), *Sequence and Space in Pompeii*, Oxford, 121–34

———. 2000a 'Systems for the disposal of waste and excreta in Roman cities; the situation in Pompeii, Herculaneum and Ostia', Raventós and Remolà 2000, 37–49

———. 2000b 'Studying Roman hygiene: the battle between the "optimists" and the "pessimists"', Jansen, G. (ed.), *Cura Aquarum in Sicilia: Proceedings of the Tenth International Congress on the History of Water Management and Hydraulic Engineering in the Mediterranean Region*, Leiden, 275–79

———. 2007 'The water system: supply and drainage', Dobbins, J. and Foss, P. (eds), *The World of Pompeii*, London

Jasny, N. 1950 'The daily bread of the ancient Greeks and Romans', *Osiris* 9, 227–53

Johnston, J.F. 1978 *Hadrian's Wall*, London

Jones, J.J. 2003 'Sources of effluence: water through Roman Lincoln', Wilson, P. (ed.), *The Archaeology of Roman Towns*, Oxford, 111–27

Jones, R. and Robinson, D. 2005 'Water, wealth and social status at Pompeii: the House of the Vestals in the first century', *American Journal of Archaeology* 109, no 4, 695–710.

Keller, D. 2005 'Social and economic aspects of glass recycling', Bruhn, J., Croxford, B. and Grigoropoulos, D. (eds), *TRAC 2004: Proceedings of the Fourteenth Annual Theoretical Roman Archaeology Conference*, Oxford, 65–78

Kent, R. 1938 *Varro: On the Latin Language Books V–VII*, Cambridge

Kenward, H.K., Allsion, E.P., Morgan, L.M., Jones, A.K. and Hutchinson, A.R. 1991 'The insect and parasite remains', McCarthy, M.R., *The Structural Sequence and Environmental Remains from Castle Street, Carlisle: Excavations 1981–2*, Cumberland Westmorland Antiquarian and Archaeological Society Research Series 5

Kenyon, K.M. 1935 'The Roman theatre at Verulamium, St Albans', *Archaeologia* 84, 213–61

Khanna, A. and Khanna, C. 2006 *Water and Sanitation in Rural Areas of Madhya Pradesh*, WaterAid India report

Knights, B.A., Dickson, C.A., Dickson, J.H. and Breeze, D.J. 1983 'Evidence concerning the Roman military diet at Bearsden, Scotland, in the 2nd century AD', *Journal of Archaeological Science* 10, 139–52

Lascaratos, J.G and Marketos, S.G. 1998 'The carbon monoxide poisoning of two Byzantine emperors', *Clinical Toxicology* 36(1&2), 103–7

Lewis, N. and Rheinhold, M. 1966 *Roman Civilization Sourcebook I: the Republic*, New York

Liebeschuetz, W. 2000 'Rubbish disposal in Greek and Roman cities', Raventós and Remolà 2000, 51–61

Loughran, D. and Pritchett, L. 1997 *Environmental Scarcity Resource Collection and the Demand for Children in Nepal*, World Bank Working Paper

Markham, G. 1613 *The English Husbandman*

Macdonald, G. 1935 'Rudolf Laur-Belart: *Vindonissa, Lager und* Vicus', *Journal of Roman Studies* 25, 247–9

MacDonald, F.J. 1982 *Crowdie and Cream: Memoirs of a Hebridean Childhood*, Aylesbury

MacGregor, A. 1985 *Bone, Antler, Ivory and Horn: the Technology of Skeletial Materials*, London

McDonough, C.M. 1999 'Forbidden to enter the *Ara Maxima*: dogs and flies or dogflies?', *Mnemosyne* 52, 464–77

McParland, L.C., Hazell, Z., Campbell, G., Collinson, M.E. and Scott, A.C. 2009 'How the Romans got themselves into hot water: temperatures and fuel types used in firing a hypocaust', *Environmental Archaeology* 14(2), 176–83

Miller, R. 1990 'Hogs and Hygiene', *Journal of Egyptian Archaeology* 76, 125–40

Moeller, W. O. 1969 'The male weavers of Pompeii', *Technology and Culture,* 10(4), 561–6

Monaghan, J. 1993 *Roman Pottery from the Fortress*, Archaeology of York 16/7

Moritz, L.A. 1958 *Grain Mills and Flour in Classical Antiquity*, Oxford

Morton Braund, S. 2004 *Juvenal and Persius*, Cambridge

Munro, J.H. 2003 'Medieval woollens: textiles, textile technology and industrial organisation, *c.* 800–1500', Jenkins, D. (ed.), *Cambridge History of Western Textiles Volume 1*, Cambridge, 181–227

Nappo, S. 1998 *Pompeii*, London

Nicholson, P.T. and Shaw, I. 2000 *Ancient Egyptian Materials and Technology*, Cambridge

Oleson, J.P. 1986 *Bronze Age, Greek and Roman Technology: a Select Annotated Bibliography*, New York

Pacitto, A.L. 1980 'Iron objects from the bottom of the well', Stead 1980, 110–6

Pdaley, T.G. 1991 *The Metalwork, Glass and Stone Objects from Carlisle Street, Carlisle: Excavations 1981–2*, Cumberland and Westmorland Antiquarian and Archaeological Society Research Series 5

Painter, K.S. 2001 *The* Insula *of the Menander at Pompeii, Volume 4: the Silver Treasure*, Oxford

Panagiotakopulu, E., Buckland, P.C. and Day, P.M., 1995 'Natural insecticides and insect repellents in antiquity: a review of the evidence', *Journal of Archaeological Science* 22, 705–10

Panagiotakopulu, E. and Buckland, P.C. 1998 '*Cimex lectularius* L., the common bed bug from Pharaonic Egypt', *Antiquity* 73, 908–11

Parsons, P. 2007 *City of the Sharp-nosed Fish*, London

Partington, J.R. and Hall, B.S. 1999 *A History of Greek Fire and Gunpowder*, Baltimore

Peña, J.T. 2007 *Roman Pottery in the Archaeological Record*, New York

Pennant, T. 1774 *A Tour in Scotland, and Voyage to the Hebrides, 1772*

Picard, L. 2001a *Restoration London*, London

———. 2001b *Dr Johnson's London*, London

Pickford, J. 1995 *Low-cost Sanitation: a Survey of Practical Experience*, London

Porter, V. 1987 *The Field Book of Country Queries*, London

Price, J. and Cottam, S. 1998 *Romano-British Glass Vessels: a Handbook*, York

Pugsley, P. 2003 *Roman Domestic Wood*, British Archaeological Report S1118

Rackham, O. 1982 'The growing and transport of timber and underwood', McGail, S. (ed.), *Wood-working Techniques Before AD 1500*, British Archaeological Report S129

Rahtz, P.A., Harden, D.B., Dunning, G.C. and Ralegh Radford, C.A. 1958 'Three post-Roman finds from the temple well at Pagans Hill, Somerset', *Medieval Archaeology* 2, 104–11

Raventós, X.D. and Remolà, J. (eds) 2000 *Sordes Urbis: la Eliminación de Residos en la Ciudad Romana*, Rome

Reedy, J. 1993 'The life of Hypatia from the Suda', *Alexandria* 2, 58

Reynolds, B. 1964 'Domestic fuels in primitive society', *Man* 64, 76–7

RIBI = Collingwood, R.G. and Wright, R.P. (eds) 1965 *Roman Inscriptions of Britain, Volume 1*, Oxford

RIBII = Frere, S.S. and Tomlin, R.S.O. (eds) 1992 *Roman Inscriptions of Britain, Volume II, Fascicule 4*, Stroud

Robinson, D. 1987 'Spice and famine food? The botanical analysis of two post-Reformation pits from Elgin, Scotland', *Circaea* 5.1, 21–7

Rook, T. 1978 'The development and operation of Roman hypocausted baths', *Journal of Archaeological Science* 5, 269–82

Roth, J.P. 1999 *The Logistics of the Roman Army at War (264 BC–AD 235)*, Leiden

Rowlandson, J. (ed.) 1998 *Women and Society in Greek and Roman Egypt*, Cambridge

Scobie, A. 1986 'Slums, sanitation and mortality in the Roman world', *Klio* 68, 399–433

Shelton, K.J. 1981 *The Esquiline Treasure*, London

Shrestha, K.B. Undated *Improved Rotary Quern: Drudgery Reducing Agricultural Equipment for Rural Women*, Nepalese Society of Agricultural Engineers Report

Shott, M.J. 1996 'Mortal pots: on use life and vessel size in the formation of ceramic assemblages', *American Antiquity* 61, 463–82

Smith, B.G. 1993 *The 'Lower Sort': Philadelphia's Laboring People, 1750–1800*, Ithaca

Smith, D. and Tetlow, E. 2009 'Insect remains', Howard-Davis, C., *The Carlisle Millennium Project Excavations in Carlisle 1998–2001, Volume 2: the Finds*, Lancaster Imprints 15

Spain, R. 2002 *A Possible Roman Tide Mill*, Kent Archaeology Papers 5

Spawforth, T. 2008 *Versailles: a Biography of a Palace*, New York

Spinazzola, V. 1953 *Pompei alla Luce degli Scavi Nuovi di Via Dell'Abbondanza (anni 1910–1923) Volume 2*, Rome

Stead, I.M. 1980 *Rudston Roman Villa*, Leeds

Stallibrass, S. 2000 'Dead dogs, dead horses: site formation processes at Ribchester Roman fort', Rowley-Conwy, P. (ed.), *Animal Bones, Human Societies*, Oxford

Strong, D. and Brown, D. 1976 *Roman Crafts*, London

Sumpter, A.B. 1990 'Pottery from Well 1', Wrathmell and Nicholson 1990, 235–45

Temkin, O. 1956 *Soranus' Gynecology*, Baltimore

Thomas, T.K. 2001 *Textiles from Karanis, Egypt in the Kelsey Museum of Archaeology*, Ann Arbor

Treggiari, S. 1976 'Jobs for women', *American Journal of Ancient History* 1, 76–104

Turner, E.G. 2007 'The Graeco-Roman branch of the Egypt Exploration Society', Bowman *et al.* 2007, 17–29

van der Veen, M. 1994 'Reports on the biological remains', Bidwell, P. and Speak, S., *Excavations at South Shields Roman Fort Volume I*, Newcastle upon Tyne

Wai-Ma, L. 1984 'Dance no more: Chinese hand laundries in Toronto', *Polyphony: Bulletin of the Multicultural History Society of Ontario*, 32–4

Walker, S. and Bierbrier, M. 1997 *Ancient Faces: Mummy Portraits from Roman Egypt*, London

Walton Rogers, P. 1997 *Textile Production at 16–22 Coppergate*, Archaeology of York 17/11

Wauthelet, M. 1998 'Urban consumption of biomass energy in Morocco', *Boiling Point* 41

White, K.D. 1970 *Roman Farming*, London

Wiedermann, T. 1981 *Greek and Roman Slavery*, London

Wild, J.P. 1967 'The *gynaeceum* at Venta and its context', *Latomus* 26, 648–76

———. 1970a *Textile Manufacture in the Northern Roman Provinces*, Cambridge

———. 1970b 'Note', in 'The copy of Diocletian's Edict on Maximum Prices from Aphrodisias in Caria', *Journal of Roman Studies* 60, 120–41

———. 1993 'The textiles', van Driel-Murray, C., Wild, J.P., Seaward, M. and Hillam, J., *Vindolanda Research Reports, Volume III: the Early Wooden Forts, Preliminary Reports on the Leather, Textiles, Environmental Evidence and Dendrochronology*, Haxham

———. 2002 'The Textile industries of Roman Britain', *Britannia* 23, 1–42

Williams, T. 2003 'Water and the Roman city: life in Roman Britain', Wilson, P. (ed.), *The Archaeology of Roman Towns*, Oxford, 242–50

Wilson, A. 2000 'Incurring the wrath of Mars: sanitation and hygiene in Roman North Africa' Jansen, G. (ed.) *Cura Aquarum in Scilia: Proceedings of the Tenth International Congress on the History of Water Management and Hydraulic Engineering in the Mediterranean Region*, Leiden, 307–12

Wilson, A. 2002 'Machines, power and the ancient economy', *Journal of Roman Studies* 92, 1–32

———. 2003 'Late antique water-mills on the Palatine', *Papers of the British School at Rome* 71, 85–109

Woodward, N. 1935 *The Rushlight* 1.4 (see www.rushlight.org/research)

Wrathmell, S. and Nicholson, A. (eds) 1990 *Dalton Parlours: Iron Age Settlement and Roman Villa*, Yorkshire Archaeology 3

Wright, L. 2004 *Warm and Snug: the History of the Bed*, Stroud

INDEX

Note: page numbers shown in **bold** indicate figures; there may also be relevant text on these pages.